Forward

Mark Rosenthal has dedicated his life to working with all types of animals. He educates, as well as entertains, audiences all over the United States. This is his second book filled with true stories that occurred throughout his career.

This book is for animal lovers everywhere. Come take a journey back throughout Mark's life, as he relates some of his most memorable stories. He promises you will not only laugh, but shed a few tears, as well.

To Juke, Isaiah & Julius,

Chapters

Chapters (continued)

The Bandit

Rasheed, one of the many raccoons we bottle raised

This story happened during a night in 1997. I don't remember the date…it isn't important. Here is some background information. We had a 220-gallon fish tank in our kitchen. It was eight-feet long and stood about five-feet off the ground. It was the first thing anyone saw when they walked into our house through our sliding glass door.

This tank housed a breeding group of African cichlids and Frontosas. Look them up; they are so cool! The aquarium was against the East wall, so you would be looking at one of the short ends when you entered our house. It was late at night, and I was watching the television in our living room with my daughter, when our two Great Danes started barking. We heard a noise coming from the kitchen, so I ran in and turned on the light.

I immediately noticed the sliding glass door was slid open about a foot. I assumed someone had broken into our house. Well, I guess I should say entered our house, since we never locked the door. I figured we didn't have to with two huge two-hundred pound dogs.

I didn't see anything amiss, so I figured someone tried to come in, opened the door and took off when our dogs started barking. I looked around and knew that whoever tried to get in couldn't have made it past the kitchen, or we would have seen them from the living room. I closed the door and locked it before going back into the living room.

About an hour later, I heard a loud noise coming from the kitchen again and one of our dogs was barking. It sounded like someone was ransacking the place. I told my daughter, Jessica, to stay in the living room while I went back to the kitchen. I turned on the light and saw nothing at all.

This time, I turned off the light, and instead of going back into the living room, I hid around the corner to see what would happen. After a couple of minutes, I heard some noise coming from behind the fish tank. This massive fish tank was on a cabinet stand that I built, and whatever was making the noise was either behind or under the stand.

I turned the light back on and still saw nothing. I grabbed a flashlight from one of the drawers and went to the right side of the fish tank to look between the tank and the wall. I shined the light and observed two eyes looking right back at me. I then heard this awful low-pitched growl. I was face-to-face with one of the largest raccoons I had ever seen, right in my kitchen!

We bottle-raise many orphaned raccoon babies every year and then teach them to fend for themselves before setting them free. Some of them we even release on our ten acres of property. I assume one of them got hungry and came up to the house to seek out food. It slid the door open with its paws and entered our house. That would explain the door being about a foot open when I checked the first time.

This raccoon must have heard the dogs bark and hid behind the fish tank. It was no longer a cute, friendly little baby...it was a completely psycho adult! I had no idea how to get it out from behind the fish tank. Water weighs eight pounds per gallon, so the weight of the water alone weighed 1,760 pounds, not including the tank and the stand. It would be physically impossible to move the aquarium. There was about enough room for one of my arms to fit behind it, but there was no way I was reaching back there blindly with an adult raccoon hiding. I would rather handle venomous snakes with my bare hands than try to mess with an adult raccoon!

I noticed a wooden broom in the corner. I grabbed it to try and prod the raccoon out. This beast grabbed the end of the broomstick and attacked it, shredding it with his teeth. It looked like we were playing tug-of-war with the broom. I finally got him to release the broom, which I think I still have somewhere and saw how badly he had destroyed it. That would have been my hand and arm, had I tried to reach back there. I'm glad I had Jessie stay in the living room.

I put my dogs in the other room and blocked off the door leading from the kitchen to the living room. I didn't want my daughter or my dogs getting hurt. Even though my dogs were huge, I believe the raccoon would have won. Again, I had no clue how I was going to get this monster raccoon out from behind the fish tank. He was still spitting, growling and hissing.

After about two hours of trying to get him to come out with various objects, I was really getting frustrated and tired. I went outside to one of our barns and brought in an animal crate. I tried to entice this beast into the carrier with all kinds of food, but he was way too smart for that. Raccoons are extremely intelligent. I eventually slid the sliding glass door all the way open, and I went to the far side of the fish tank. I got a different broom and put the bristle end behind the aquarium. I couldn't see what I was doing because there was no room, so I started moving the broom around to try and scare him out.

Well, I still had the flashlight back there and either the flashlight or the broom (or both) finally got to him, and I saw him run out the far side of the aquarium. I had a 50/50 shot…either he would make a left and go further into the kitchen, or he would go straight and exit our house. Luckily, he ran outside, I shut the door, and that door has been locked every night since!

Worst Vacation Ever

Tinker & Trip on the couch at Houghton Lake

I was raising Jessica, my daughter, by myself, when I met Diane, my future wife, in February, 2004. Jessica and I were on our way to Houghton Lake in August with Tinker, her 205-pound Great Dane, and a two-week-old greater bush baby. Tinker was one of the best dogs we ever had. Our biggest problem with him was he loved to steal food off the counter and kitchen table. If it was edible, or not, he would eat it. Keep in mind that I had only known Diane for about four months when this story occurred.

I was one of the first people in the United States to successfully breed greater bush babies, which are lesser primates native to Africa. At the time, I was bottle feeding a two-week-old baby with Similac, the formula I use. It's a white powder that I mix with water. I buy it in bulk, two-pound containers, because I use it on all of our primate babies.

Jessie and I brought this baby with us and set his crate on a heating pad in our cabin, since he was too young to regulate his own body temperature. I also brought an unopened canister of Similac and a baby bottle. I mixed up the formula and fed her before heading out to my parents' cabin with Jessie. My parents have a cabin that is about ¼ mile from where we stay, and we go there a lot. I placed the baby bottle in the fridge, since it had to be kept cold and left the large canister of powder on the table.

I called Diane and asked if she and her daughter, Samantha, wanted to meet us up there. She said, "Yes," and they left right away. Jessica and I were going to sleep in the bedroom, since there were two beds; Diane and Sam were going to sleep on the sofa in the living room, which converted into a bed.

Jessie and I were at my parents' cabin when Diane and Sam arrived around two o'clock. Diane called me when she got off the freeway, and I gave her directions to my parents' cabin. After greeting us, Diane asked for directions to my cabin, so she could take their luggage and freshen up. Sam stayed at my parents' cabin with us.

Diane was gone for over an hour, and I was wondering what was taking so long. Well, here is what happened. Whoever is reading this book right now will find this incredibly humorous, but trust me, Diane didn't!

Tinker, our "chow hound," took the canister of powdered Similac off the table and chewed it open. He then ate the whole thing…almost TWO POUNDS! The powder that wasn't eaten was all over the cabin. Now, that much would make anyone sick…especially a dog. It went right through him and made him violently ill. He had no way to get outside and he couldn't hold it in any longer. He had massive, explosive diarrhea all over the cabin, and I mean ALL OVER THE CABIN…on the couch, on the carpet, on the walls, on the wood floor, in the bathroom and everywhere else you could imagine.

The good news was that I was at my parents' cabin with Jessie and Sam and had no idea what was going on. The bad news, at least for Diane, was that she went to my cabin to put her suitcase away. She opened the door and started gagging. Not only did the smell hit her, but she saw Tinker covered in this brown/white diarrhea. She then noticed my cabin. She said there was powder and diarrhea from one end of the cabin to the other. I would have expected her to close the door and come back to my parents' cabin, but she was so cool.

She immediately took Tinker into the lake to clean him off and then placed him on the porch. This remarkable woman went into my cabin and proceeded to clean up the diarrhea and powder. What made it even more problematic was that Similac is a powder, so every time Diane used wet paper towels to wipe it up, it would just form a paste and make it even more difficult.

She eventually came back to my parents' cabin and told us what had happened. There wasn't much left to clean by the time we returned to my cabin, but we had to drive to a laundry mat to wash the couch cushion covers and the carpet runners. The smell was still in the air, but everything looked all right when we got back, for the most part. We learned our lesson, so from then on, we always put everything on top of the refrigerator where Tinker couldn't get it.

Cirque Du Soleil

Widget   Tank

It was Father's Day weekend, June 2004. I had only known Diane for four months now, and I was performing at the National Strawberry Festival in downtown Belleville. They hired me every year, and this was going to be the first time Diane had ever seen me perform.

I arrived early in the morning to set up the stage, because I had four performances that afternoon and evening. I had forgotten one of my magic tricks at home, and I also needed a different crate for Tank.

Tank is a giant six-banded armadillo. "Tank" was the perfect name for this remarkable creature, because he was built like an armored vehicle. Tank is Diane's favorite animal, and he still lives in our sanctuary, more than fifteen years since I acquired him.

Tank was almost impossible to contain. He would break out of anything when I tried to transport him. His claws are amazing. Picture this: If I was to bend over and place him on the grass and then stand back up, he would already be underground by the time I bent back down again!

This type of armadillo is native to Paraguay, where they burrow and live underground. This was my first time bringing Tank to a show and I had no idea that he was an escape artist. I placed him in a hard plastic dog carrier and drove him to the festival. He had already escaped by the time I arrived. He completely destroyed the carrier, and I had no way to contain him.

I had to let him run loose in the back of my van, until I could figure out what to do. Even though Diane and her daughter lived about 25 minutes away, I called and asked if she could do me a favor. I asked if she could stop by my house on the way to the festival and pick up the magic trick that I had left in the house. I also asked if she could go to my sanctuary and find me another crate in which to put Tank. She said, "No problem, see you in a little while."

Here is a little background information that is necessary for this story: In addition to my three giant dogs, three exotic animals lived in my house. The first one was Ben, a fennec fox, the world's smallest fox. Next, we had Johari, a greater bush baby, a lesser primate that resembles a small monkey and is native to

Africa. Finally, we had Widget, a large black and white ruffed lemur, native to Madagascar, which are the largest and most endangered of all lemurs.

I bottle-raised all of these animals since they were babies, and all three were members of my family. They even ate whatever Jessica and I had for dinner. There is a room between our kitchen and living room where they were all housed. Diane had met all of these animals a few times, but didn't really know them. All of this information is pertinent to this story.

Diane drove to my sanctuary and found a pretty sturdy carrier for Tank. She then arrived at my house to retrieve the magic prop I had left behind. I never locked our door because nobody was ever going to get past our three dogs. What Diane didn't know was that Widget had opened her cage and was in the kitchen looking for food. Widget jumped right on top of Diane's head as soon as she opened the sliding glass door. Widget was the friendliest animal I have ever owned, and she had never tried to bite anyone. I trusted her completely…anyone could handle her.

Diane didn't know this and she had no idea what to do. Widget had a habit that she only did with females. She would rub her back end on human females' heads to mark her territory. I know it sounds funny, but it's 100% true. She never did this to me, my dad, or any other guys…only women. Diane has a beautiful head of auburn hair, and it must have been a sight to behold…a large black and white monkey rubbing her hind end on Diane's beautiful red head. Diane couldn't get Widget off of her head and didn't know what to do. There was nobody else home and Diane couldn't go back outside with this monkey on her head. In addition, Diane didn't know if she was going to be urinated on or attacked!

She tried reaching up to grab Widget, and she tried leaning over to get Widget to jump off, both to no avail. Widget kept rubbing her butt on Diane's head this whole time. Diane went into the other room, with Widget still on her head, and tried to get Widget to go back into her cage. Johari and Widget were jealous of each other, because they always wanted to run around the house. We only let one of them out at a time.

Johari reached through the bars of her cage and grabbed Diane. Picture this…Diane didn't really know Widget or Johari. They were both trying to grab each other, Widget was rubbing her butt on Diane's head and Ben was screaming to try and get Diane's attention. Diane finally bent over and Widget jumped back into her cage. I don't know how she managed to do it, but it worked. She got my magic trick and left right away, so I could have it before my first show started.

She arrived at the Strawberry Festival and got out of her car. I asked her what took so long. I then asked her why she smelled so badly. She hadn't had time to wash her hair before she left my house, and it smelled like Widget. Diane is a real trooper and still married me after everything she had been through.

Frank, my brother-in-law, is a welder by trade, and he welded me a stainless steel, escape-proof armadillo carrier that I still use to this day.

Motel Madness

I was performing 12 shows in the Flint, Michigan area on January 18 & 19, 2012; six assemblies each day. I needed to get a hotel room, since it was snowing, and I didn't want to drive back and forth both days. I always try to reserve a room at a Red Roof Inn, because they allow animals. I had Trip with me, our 200-pound Great Dane, along with quite a few exotic animals.

I finished my first day's six shows and arrived at the motel around 3:30 p.m. when I checked in. The counter lady said it was good that I had a reservation, because they were completely booked and had no available rooms. I always request a room on the ground level, so I don't have to carry all my animals' cages up any stairs. I was really dirty and tired and just wanted to take a shower and grab some dinner. I left at five in the morning, performed all day; now, I was ready for some food.

I drove to my room, opened the door and a heat wave hit me. It had to be over 100 degrees, without exaggerating. It was worse than a sauna. I tried to turn off the heater, but found it was broken. There was no way I could stay in a room that hot with all of my animals, so I drove back to the office. I complained that the room was way too hot. The lady apologized and said the heater was not working properly. I told her I figured that out and there was no way I could stay in that room. I should mention that I knew this was a one-star motel, but I figured I was only staying for one night, so how bad could it be? I wasn't there for fun, just to get some rest.

It was at this point I was told there were no other rooms, and all the other hotels were at full capacity, as well. This lady acted like she was used to this...no apology at all. She said there was nothing she could do, so I asked to speak to her manager. Service people usually co-operate more when you ask for a manager, because they don't want to get in trouble. She said she would check again and, lo and behold, she found me another room.

She said she could move someone else around, who hadn't arrived yet, and I could have their room. Keep in mind that I arrived at 3:30 in the afternoon and it was now 3:45. I drove to the next room and was happy, because the room was at a reasonable temperature. I brought all my animals in and unpacked all of my toiletries. I took Trip outside to go to the bathroom, and we went back into the room to relax for a few minutes before leaving to get some dinner.

I turned on the sink, and nothing came out. I tried both the hot and the cold. Nothing. Not only couldn't I wash my hands, but I couldn't even give Trip any water, let alone the other animals. I then figured I could just use the shower to give water to the animals and to wash. I knew this was the last available room, so I decided to make the best of it. I turned on the shower and got the same result. No water at all.

I had some wet wipes in my van that I used to wipe my hands. I then packed up all my stuff, turned the heat on in the van for the animals and loaded everything back in. I drove back to the front desk, told the lady that I had no water and that I had already unpacked all my stuff.

I asked what was going on and she nonchalantly informed me that the whole motel had no water. She then told me they have been working on it for a few hours. I asked her why she didn't tell me that when I checked in. She said that none of the rooms had water and that it should be back on in less than one hour. She said there was nothing she could do (again), and assured me the water would be back on shortly. I told her that I would go back to the room and wait, since it was now too late for me to drive all the way home. I drove back to the room (again), brought everything in and unpacked (again), tried the water (again) only with the same result...nothing.

I drove to a nearby 7-Eleven and purchased a gallon of water for Trip and the mammals that were with me. It was now a little after 5:00 p.m. when the water should have been back on. I keep waiting. Six p.m. and still nothing. I called the front desk and asked what was going on, since I was told the water would be back on by five. She said that quite a few people had already left, and there was nothing she could do. She then informed me that she now had no idea when, or if, the water would be turned back on. I told her this was crazy, so I decided that I would go to a restaurant to wash my hands, have dinner, and then check the water one last time when I returned. If the water wasn't back on, then I was going to pack everything up (again), drive all the way home, just to drive all the way back the following morning. I ate dinner and returned around 7:30 p.m., only to discover the water still wasn't back on.

I called the front desk and asked what was going on (again). I explained to this lady that I arrived at 3:30 and was told the water would be back on by 4:30. It's now almost 8:00 p.m., and I still have no water. She apologized, saying she didn't know what to tell me. She had no clue when it was going to be turned back on. She sounded like a broken record. I said I was going to check out and get my money back, since I couldn't stay there. I was extremely upset, because I was tired and now had a long drive in front of me. As I was packing up my stuff for the third time, I heard the water start running in the bathtub. I had left the faucet open to hear if it came back on. It was now 8:15 p.m. I finally had water, so I washed up and brushed my teeth, deciding to stay the night. Wait, we're not done yet, as nothing went right in this motel.

Trip had a thyroid problem and needed medicine twice daily. I had been giving it to him for over three years now. The easiest way to give him his pills (two in the morning and two in the evening) was to hide them in canned dog food. It was much easier than opening his mouth and forcing them down his throat. This room had a refrigerator and a microwave, so I placed the open can of dog food in the fridge after giving him his pills. I awakened the following morning, took a shower, brushed my teeth, packed everything up and opened the fridge to get the dog food for Trip's pills. I then discovered the refrigerator was broken also. The open can of dog food was frozen solid! I stopped at a store on my way to the first school and purchased a pack of hot dogs. I hid Trip's pills in one and put the rest in my cooler.

You're probably laughing while reading this, but I didn't find any of it funny. The only good thing to come out of it was this story. I've stayed in Flint many times since, but I've never returned to that motel!

Alley-Oop

I received a phone call a few years ago from Becky, a police officer in Woodhaven, Michigan. Trenton doesn't have an animal control in their city, so all of their calls are referred to the Woodhaven Police Department. I've helped them out many times over the years, and they needed my assistance again.

Becky said some people were standing on their front porch the previous night when they saw a three-foot alligator walking down the sidewalk toward their house. OK, that's not normal…especially in Trenton, Michigan. One of the women called the police, and two officers showed up and corralled this alligator into a crate and brought it to their police station. The officers placed it in a holding cell until Becky arrived in the morning. She called me and asked if I would pick up this alligator from the police station. I said, "Of course," and I left for the 30-minute drive.

I arrived to an incredible scene. It was like a three-ring circus. It seemed word got out, and the media was all over the place. Reporters from the Detroit News, the Detroit Free Press and the local paper were all there, in addition to, TV crews from NBC, ABC and Fox News. I also received phone calls for interviews from the Associated Press later that day. I was at the police station giving one interview after another for over two hours. It was crazy, all because this small alligator was walking down the sidewalk in Trenton. I gave all the interviews; you can still find some of them by searching online for "alligator, Trenton, Michigan." There's even an article written by the Los Angeles Times. The story didn't end there.

Becky called me a few days later and asked if I still had the alligator. Whenever I help out local police agencies and rescue an animal, I always quarantine it for a minimum of two weeks, just in case they find the owner, or if they need me to appear with the animal in court, depending on the case. I won't try to place the animal in a zoo or other animal facility until I hear that I have the OK, or until at least two weeks have passed.

Becky told me I wouldn't believe this. She said the alligator's owner came forward and called her, wanting it back. I told her she had to be joking, since alligators are against the law to own as pets. This man said it was his gator and that it was sunning itself in his backyard when he went inside to get the phone. The alligator somehow escaped his yard, and now he wanted it back. Becky told him he couldn't have it back, because it was against the law. He retorted,

"We'll see about that." He hung up without leaving his name, phone number or address.

Becky received a phone call later that afternoon from an attorney who said he was now representing this man who wants his "pet" back. Becky took down all the information and then called me. It seemed this man, who owned the alligator, also owned a restaurant in Southgate, Michigan and was planning on displaying this alligator in a cage in the middle of his restaurant to draw in customers.

Becky had already explained the laws about owning crocodilians to the attorney, and after doing some research, realized his hands were tied. Becky then got his client's information and went over to this man's house. She issued him two citations, one for an animal running at large and one for harboring an illegal animal. He also had to pay his attorney fees, court costs and the fees for four officers' overtime pay.

This moron had to pay a tremendous fine and didn't get his alligator back, all because he called an attorney to fight his battle. I've assisted in too many alligator rescues to count, but none this well publicized.

I guess it was a slow day for news.

Cruisin' Down the Highway

Here's another police story that occurred in 2010. I received a phone call from the Sumpter Township Police Department. The officer needed my help with a snake. He had no idea what kind it was and said he had it in a pillow case in the back of his squad car. I said, "Of course I would help," and I had him meet me in my driveway. I asked him what the story was with this snake; here is what he told me. This is one of the most bizarre stories I've ever heard.

It seems like a man was driving East on I-94, going right past the Detroit Metropolitan Airport in Romulus. He had a young child in a car seat in the back seat, and his windows were open. His child wanted Dad to get one of his toys that was on the front passenger floor. There was nobody sitting there, just a bunch of toys on the floor. This man leaned over while he was driving and was feeling around on the floor for this toy, all the while trying to stay focused on the road.

He grabbed what he thought was a toy and realized it wasn't...when it moved. What he had actually grabbed was a four-foot python! This man had Ophidiophobia; an intense, irrational fear of snakes.

Once he realized what was in his hand, he freaked out, and his car started swerving across the freeway. He almost crashed into numerous cars before pulling over onto the right shoulder. One of the cars behind him followed him off the road to see what was wrong. The man following the car thought the man driving in front of him had suffered a heart attack or blew out a tire.

The first driver jumped out of his car and started screaming. He left his child in the back seat with the snake loose in the car. This man was freaking out, and the second driver calmly asked him what had happened. He was told that someone had apparently thrown a snake into his open window. He had no idea where it was, if it was venomous, or if there were other snakes in his car. Luckily for him, the nice man who stopped to help had pet snakes of his own. He opened up the passenger side front door and brought out some kind of boa or python. The nice man checked the rest of the car and didn't find any other snakes. He secured the snake in a pillow case that he had in his trunk. You might think that is weird, but I always travel with pillow cases in my van, in case I encounter any snakes.

The first driver was still shaken up and didn't want to give his name or any other information. He got back in his car without so much as a thank you and took off down the freeway. The second driver called the Romulus Police and told them what had happened. They, in turn, called the Sumpter Township Police, and they called me.

The only assumption we came up with is the driver was a drug dealer. We have a lot of them in

Detroit, and he probably crossed the wrong people. They must have known about his fear of snakes, so they either put it in his window, which was open, before he got in the car, or tossed it into his window while driving, hoping to cause an accident. It makes sense, because the driver didn't stick around for the police or even thank the other driver for stopping to help.

I reached into the pillow case after retrieving it from the squad car and identified the snake as a ball python. These snakes are native to Africa and can't survive in the wild in Michigan, which is how we know it didn't just crawl into his car. I still have that ball python, and I guarantee it's doing much better than that guy. I'll bet he hasn't slept through the night since that day. What a weird story.

Buckwheat

A couple photos of Buckwheat

This is one of the saddest, most disturbing rescues we've ever done. I received a phone call in 2009 from a lady who I'll call, "Mary." She told me she had attended one of my shows and looked me up on line to check my credentials. She needed to find a home for her pet monkey, a weeper capuchin. Weeper capuchins were the organ grinder monkeys seen in old movies. Most of them were white-faced or cinnamon capuchins. Mary said her monkey's name was Buckwheat and that he was 26-years-old. I asked her what the story was on Buckwheat and why she no longer wanted him.

Mary said that she and her husband couldn't have children, so they bought Buckwheat 26 years ago and treated him as their own child. They bottle-raised him, diapered him, clothed him and took him everywhere they went. He accompanied them to restaurants and movies; he even loved to shop at K-Mart. He was the son they never had. I asked her why they were getting rid of Buckwheat after all these years,

29

and Mary said Buckwheat had been housed in a tiny birdcage in their kitchen for the past 23 years. I found this so cruel. I asked her why and she said that Buckwheat bit off two of her fingers when he was three-years old.

In my educated opinion, monkeys are not pets! They are extremely dangerous and dirty animals. They are also very strong and intelligent. I know the monkeys you see on television seem friendly and cute. Please keep in mind that those few seconds they are on TV can actually take up to a week to film. I know…I've done it! Monkeys are not pets! In my opinion, it's not fair to keep them in a house. I'm not against keeping exotic animals as pets, but certain ones can't be domesticated and are dangerous, as well as, illegal.

Bearded dragons, ball pythons, boa constrictors, most geckos, smaller tortoises…these are all wonderful pets. Larger primates, alligators and large constrictors just don't belong in a house, especially where there are children present. One of the other chapters in this book tells the story when I rescued a cobra from a man's trailer, where he lived with his girlfriend and two young kids! OK, back to Buckwheat's story.

Mary said that Buckwheat just attacked her and bit off two of the fingers on her right hand. I guess either something scared him, or he reached sexual maturity. I asked Mary why Buckwheat was in the kitchen, and she said that ever since he had bitten her fingers off, they no longer trusted him and didn't want to place him with anyone else. They didn't know what to do, so they kept him locked up inside a birdcage in their kitchen. Mary said when company came over, she would tell them not to make eye contact with Buckwheat, not to go in the kitchen, not to laugh or talk loudly…nothing that would stress out Buckwheat.

Keep in mind, this highly intelligent primate had been locked in a three-foot-square birdcage for the past 23 years with very little human interaction, no attention and no enrichment whatsoever. The only interaction he received was when they fed him once a day. I asked Mary how they cleaned his cage and she told me Buckwheat loved water, so they took his cage outside with him in it and used the garden hose on high (jet spray) to clean the bottom of his cage. That alone probably scared the heck out of this poor guy.

I then asked what made her decide to call me now, after 23 years. She told me she was recently diagnosed with cancer and not doing well, and she didn't know what to do with Buckwheat. Mary said she attended the grand opening of a veterinary clinic where I happened to be performing, and she thought I would be perfect for Buckwheat. I told her I would be happy to take Buckwheat in temporarily, while I located a permanent home for him at a licensed zoo. I let Mary know I would definitely not be keeping Buckwheat, since it wasn't fair to house him in such a small cage. I didn't have a reason to keep him permanently, since I would never be able to trust him near anyone.

I called a friend at the University of Michigan's Biomedical Research Lab and explained we were taking in a capuchin. I asked if she had any large primate cages that we could borrow. She told me we could have one for free, as long as I drove down and picked it up. I'm glad I brought my trailer because this cage was heavy duty. It was made to house a chimpanzee… six-feet-tall by four-feet-wide, stainless steel, escape proof and weighed well over 300 pounds. It had locks and a specially-made sliding door, which made it safe for me to give Buckwheat food and water. It was much bigger than what Buckwheat had been used to, and I couldn't wait to transfer him into it. I loaded this cage onto our trailer and drove it back to our sanctuary. We brought it in and were now ready for our new arrival.

Mary, her husband and Buckwheat made the six-hour drive to us the following weekend. Buckwheat was absolutely gorgeous and had the sweetest, yet saddest, eyes. My wife and I fell in love with him the second our eyes met. Buckwheat was in a small birdcage, and the only thing in there with him was a blue bucket that hung from the top. Buckwheat loved that bucket and slept in it every night. I decided to transfer the bucket into his new cage, so he would have something familiar. I gave him a banana to keep busy, and managed to get the bucket out without him escaping. He was very leery of me, and I knew how dangerous he was. I hung this bucket in his new cage and now had to figure out how to get him in there without him attacking me. He didn't know me, he had already bitten off two of his "mom's" fingers and I needed to make sure we were both safe.

I placed some marshmallows in the bottom of the new cage, slid the door up and locked it in an open position. I turned Buckwheat's birdcage sideways and opened the door, hoping he would just walk into the primate cage. It couldn't have gone any smoother. He climbed into the new cage, filled both hands with marshmallows and climbed into his bucket to eat them.

I felt so sorry for him that I actually started to cry. How could anyone keep this amazing animal locked up inside a birdcage in a kitchen for 23 years? Keep in mind, a capuchin's life span is 60-80 years, and if Mary hadn't been diagnosed with cancer, Buckwheat would have spent an addition 40-60 years in this cage.

Buckwheat became one of our favorite animals. We only had him for about one month, but he has a permanent spot in our hearts. I would visit Buckwheat's cage first, whenever I went to our sanctuary, to say hi. He actually looked forward to seeing me, or so it seemed. I never reached into his cage, because I couldn't trust him. I brought him treats every day and would hand them to him through the cage bars. He would grab them immediately. He would then reach through the bars and hold my hand with one of his while he ate the treats. I would sit and talk to him, and he seemed to listen.

One day my wife, who is an amazing singer, came out to the sanctuary to see Buckwheat. Diane loved Buckwheat and also brought him treats. She started singing, "You Are My Sunshine." Buckwheat loved it so much that he put his little hands over his heart and started swaying to the music. He proceeded to do this every time she would sing to him. It was truly amazing to see Buckwheat enjoy something so much.

It didn't take long for me to find Buckwheat a permanent home at a zoo in Kansas. I decided to drive him all the way down there…thirteen hours each way. I arrived at the zoo, and we transferred Buckwheat to his new, permanent home. I said my good-byes and drove back to Michigan, thinking of Buckwheat the whole way back. I called soon after to see how he was doing, and I was told that he was adjusting just fine. He was now living with 13 other capuchins and was able to go outside whenever he wanted. They had a partition built into his indoor pen that opened up into a fenced outdoor area. He was finally able to enjoy being outside for the first time in over 23 years. I was ecstatic!

I still think about him often, and we all miss him, but we are content knowing that he's in a much better place and finally happy. I still call the zoo every now and then to check up on Buckwheat. They love him, just like we do.

Gawk at the Hawk

Broad winged hawk we rescued

I received a phone call a couple years back from the principal at Belleville High School. She said one of the students had driven into their parking lot and parked his pick-up truck. When he got out, he noticed a large bird in the bed (the back) of his truck. It must have landed there and now either couldn't get out or didn't want to get out. He said it looked like the bird, which he thought was a falcon or hawk, couldn't fly and the principal wanted to know if I would come out and help.

I packed up my gear and drove to the school, not expecting to find the bird still there. I assumed it would be long gone by now. I saw a group of people waiting for me in the parking lot. They directed me to the truck; I got out and peeked into the back. Sure enough, there was a hawk standing there. I knew I had no chance of catching this bird with a net, because the pick-up truck was so high off the ground. I put my special gloves on that I use when handling my giant

Eurasian eagle owls. I knew I only had one chance to jump over the side and grab the bird before it would get away. I was worried that this bird was injured and that it would try to fly off. If it couldn't fly, it might flutter or jump out of the truck and be hard to catch in the parking lot.

I snuck up on the side of the truck, and lightning fast, I jumped over the side and got lucky. I grabbed the hawk without too much of a struggle. I knew it was a hawk and not a falcon, but I had no idea what kind it was. I had never seen one of these before. Its talons were huge, and I was smart to wear the gloves. I placed it in a carrier that I had brought with me and drove it back to our sanctuary. I then went online to try and identify this magnificent bird. I discovered it was a broad winged hawk. They are pretty common in Michigan…I had just never seen one. They prey on other birds and small rodents. I drove it to the Birmingham Veterinary Clinic where it was X-rayed. Dr. Fernandez found no fractured bones in the wings, and the legs seemed fine as well. Dr. Fernandez gave me some antibiotics, in case of infection, and I brought the hawk back to our sanctuary. I set it up in a cage to try and nurse it back to good health.

I don't know how many of you have ever tried to administer antibiotics to a wild hawk, but I'll let you in on a little secret…it's not easy! I crushed up the pills, diluted them in some water and injected it into frozen mice, which I thawed first. I would then toss one in for the hawk to eat. I had to repeat this four times a day for ten days. I hoped the hawk would get the medicine this way, instead of me having to stress it out by grabbing it and forcing the pills down its throat.

The hawk was extremely lethargic for the first few days. It drank some water but only picked at the mice. I could see it was getting progressively better daily, and by the fourth day, it was eating every mouse I put in its cage. After about one month, I decided it was time to release this hawk back into the wild where it belonged. I needed to see if it could fly first, because I didn't want to just let it go outside, only to find out it couldn't, having to catch it again. It's always such a wonderful feeling to set an animal free that we rehabilitated. I opened its cage door in our sanctuary and this hawk just stared at me for a few seconds. It then hopped to the cage door and flew out. Now, I hadn't thought about what I would do if it could fly, which it did. I now had to catch a loose hawk in our sanctuary! It took me about half an hour, but I finally managed to catch it in a net and place it in a carrier. It was time to be released.

Diane, James (our son, who was three at the time) and Jessica (our oldest daughter) all went outside to set this beautiful creature free. Diane had the camcorder ready; I told Jamie to say good-bye to the hawk. I put on my special gloves and got out the hawk. My plan was to just open my hands and spread my arms, letting the hawk take flight. We all got ready, Diane turned on the camcorder, Jamie said good-bye, and it was the coolest thing...she took off and flew high up into a nearby tree. She stopped and looked back at us before flying to a different branch. It was at this point that we knew she could fly and was going to be all right. She stayed in this tree for about two hours before flying off for good.

Another satisfying rescue!

Survivor

I almost made it onto the second season of the TV show, "Survivor." I got as far as the producers telling me to get a passport. I loved the first season so much, when Richard Hatch won, that I decided to try out for the second season. I filled out all of the required forms, which were over 15 pages! I then had to submit an audition tape. I wanted to make sure I sent in something original...humorous, yet also showing me working fearlessly with the animals.

I had a friend with a video camera on hand to record the tape. The criteria was that I had 90 seconds to introduce myself, state my age, explain why I should be chosen for the show and say a little bit about myself.

Here was my original idea. I set up a child's playpen in my living room placing a realistic baby doll inside. I then took one of my 15-foot albino Burmese pythons and wrapped her around the baby in the playpen. I wanted my buddy to only film me from the neck up because I didn't want anyone to see what was behind me on the floor. He started the camera rolling while I stated, "Hi, my name is Mark Rosenthal and I am 38 years old. I live in Belleville, Michigan. I should be on Survivor because I am fearless and would compete in any and all challenges. I've been working with exotics my whole life."

I went on and on, while my buddy panned the camera out to show a bigger picture. At the same time, he started the tape recorder, which was set to play a baby crying. As he panned out the camera, you could hear me yell, "My baby…My baby," as I ran over to the playpen and picked up the baby (doll). I again yelled, "Oh, my baby," as I threw the doll over my shoulder onto the floor. I reached in and picked up the python saying, "My baby!" I then turned to the camera, introduced my python to everyone watching, saying she was my baby. The video then faded to black.

Well, the producers liked it so much that one of them called and informed me that I was a finalist and that I needed to get a valid passport. I was overjoyed, but my dream of being a contestant never came to fruition. I didn't make the final cut, which worked out for the best because I ended up fracturing my left tibia in October of 2001. I wouldn't have been able to compete anyway, because I was laid up in a wheelchair for eight months. You can read that story in my first book.

Strike Out

I headlined two sold-out shows on February 26, 2011 at the Macomb Center for Performing Arts in Clinton Township, Michigan. They went great; I even got to debut my first book. I signed over 700 of them that day! I sat there for two hours after each performance to autograph books, take photos and meet everyone. The line was around the building, and it's something I'll never forget. It was awesome!

Everything went according to plan, except for a couple minor mishaps. I was in my dressing room, making sure everything was ready for my first show, when one of my nephews and brother-in-law walked in. I took them into the other dressing room, where the animals were being kept and told them to wait by the door, while I checked on my eight-foot forest cobra.

This highly venomous cobra usually went to the bathroom whenever I placed him into his crate; I needed to make sure he hadn't gone on the way to the theater. I unhinged one end and slowly lifted it to peek in, when the cobra flew out and tried to bite me. He came so close that I actually felt his breath on my right thumb and even had to check my hand to see if I had been bitten! My nephew and brother-in-law still talk about it to this day. It just proves that, not only do you have to really know what you are doing in my business, but you have to be a little lucky as well.

On the Ropes

Grasshopper, our very first baby Greater Bushbaby

Another mishap that occurred at the Macomb Center for The Performing Arts happened during my first show. I had two greater bush babies flown in from Sea World the previous week, and I really wanted to bring one of them. People always love them, because they are so adorable. Neither one was extremely friendly, but one of them, Mocha, was definitely friendlier than the other. I worked with him during the week before the show and placed him in a carrier that morning with no problems. I checked on him before the show, even letting him run around my dressing room.

When it came time to bring him out, I had one of my employees bring the carrier on stage to place it on one of the tables. I explained to the audience what I was going to bring out. Then I opened up the crate to let Mocha jump onto my shoulder. He couldn't have behaved any better. There were five different cameramen filming both performances and there were thousands of people in attendance. Both shows were also shown on a giant screen behind me, so everyone seated in the balcony could see. Mocha looked great on the screen, as I could see him out of the corner of my eye. I proceeded to walk around the stage to give everyone a better look. When I was done showing and talking about him, I leaned over his crate, hoping he would jump back into it. Mocha had other ideas. This is when everything went horribly wrong!

I can pretty much guarantee that anyone who has ever performed with animals has had something not go according to plan. Mocha decided that it was play time, so he ran across the table and jumped onto the stage floor, where he proceeded to run off the side of the stage. He leaped onto one of the ropes that is used to open and close the curtains and started climbing up. I knew if he made it to the top, he would disappear into the rafters. We would never catch him.

After dealing with animals for as long as I have, I knew that I only had one shot before he was gone. I ran off stage, leaving thousands of people wondering what was going on. I jumped up just as Mocha was about out-of-reach. I got lucky! I grabbed him and brought him back down. I was talking to the crowd this whole time, because I had a microphone pinned on me. I assured them this was all planned and everything was fine. I then brought Mocha back out to an ovation and placed him back in his carrier.

Whew…disaster averted!

See Ya' Later Alligator

Me & Beefy T in 2009   Beefy T Bad Boy in 2013

The last thing that happened from the Macomb Center for The Performing Arts occurred on my way home. I drove by myself with all of my animals, magic tricks, shirts, stuffed animals and books. The animals were in my heated van, and everything else was in my trailer. My family and employees all met me there. It was a 90-minute drive from my house in normal weather conditions. It started snowing during my first show, and it was a blizzard by the time I was all packed up at around 8:00 p.m.

I called my wife while I was en route to make sure she had arrived home safely. She had left with our son right after the second performance. There are only two animals that terrify Diane: giant snakes and alligators. Those of you who have read my first book remember the story about Beefy-T Bad Boy. He was a large alligator we rescued from Northville Township years ago. I won't repeat it…you can read about it in my first book. Anyway, there's a reason I mentioned Beefy-T.

Beefy-T Bad Boy was with me at the Macomb Center.   I had him secured in a large Rubbermaid container in the back of my van during the long ride home.   I had a few boxes of books on top of his locked carrier to make it almost impossible for him to escape. He is about seven-feet long and weighs between 150-200 pounds.   He always got everyone's attention at my shows.   I only bring him out when I'm either on stage or on a TV show, due to his large size.

Anyway, while I was telling Diane how great I thought everything went, something told me to look down to my right.   I saw Beefy-T's large head on the floor right next to my right leg.   He somehow escaped from his crate and crawled up to the front of the van. He was just lying there, right next to me.   I remained as calm as could be.   I learned years ago that screaming and jumping doesn't accomplish anything.

While still on the phone with my wife, I asked, "Hey Honey, guess what I'm looking at right now?"

She replied, "What?"

I said, "Beefy-T.   He's lying right beside me!" Well, Diane wasn't happy at all, and she proceeded to let me know it.   I decided I would just let him lay there for the rest of the drive.   It had been a long day.   I didn't want to pull over in the snow and try to put him back in his carrier.   I assumed he wouldn't attack me if I didn't give him a reason, and there was no one else in any danger since I was by myself.   The only problem I could anticipate was if he crawled forward anymore and interfered with my gas or brake pedals.

I made it home, almost three hours later, and Beefy-T was still right next to me. My wife met me at our sanctuary to help carry the animals inside. I had been gone all day and still needed to feed and water everyone. I had left my van running, because it was cold outside and the heat was on for the animals still in the van.

I hate to keep referring to my first book, but I need to once again. The longest chapter pertained to the animal thefts that occurred at our sanctuary in 2007. We were broken into twice, and many of our animals were stolen. I still haven't slept through the night since then. I'm always worried that these losers will come back, even though I know they served time in jail and our sanctuary is now like a fortress.

Back to the story. Diane and I were carrying animals in and putting them away when we both heard my van engine start to rev. Someone was pressing down on the gas pedal; each time they were revving it more and more. I realized a lot of our prized animals were still in the van, and someone was about to steal them again, in MY van this time! I had already unhooked the trailer, so the van would be easy to drive off.

The van was pointed right at our in-ground swimming pool. The pool was surrounded by a wrought iron fence. I immediately stopped what I was doing and ran across the sanctuary towards the door nearest my van. I didn't wait for my wife, who was behind me. I wanted to catch whoever was stealing my van! I opened the sanctuary door and ran around to the driver's door of my van. The engine was revving as high as it could go, but I couldn't see anybody in the driver's seat.

I opened the door and saw Beefy-T Bad Boy. He had climbed further up and his head was now under the dash with the upper third of his body resting on the gas pedal. He was stuck and couldn't move. Had his tail hit the gear shift, the van would have crashed into the railing and proceeded into the pool! I tried to get Beefy-T unstuck, but he was firmly wedged into place. I had no idea what to do. It had been a very long day. I had just driven three hours home in a blizzard. I still had animals to take care of, and now this. I had to think quickly, so I turned off the ignition. At least now the engine would stop revving and it couldn't accidentally be shifted into gear.

It took me about 40 minutes to get this monster alligator unstuck. I picked him up, which was no easy task because of his weight, and there was no way Diane was helping! I then carried him to his indoor pen. Diane held the door to our sanctuary open for me. That's asking a lot because of her fear of alligators. I went back outside once we were all done taking care of the animals and started my van to drive home. It was making a weird noise and wasn't driving properly. I thought that maybe I had hit something during my drive home, never thinking it could have something to do with Beefy-T. The following Monday morning I took my van to a friend who owned an auto repair shop.

John, the owner, told me he would call after he looked at it. He called me a few hours later and asked what had happened. I hadn't told him about the alligator until I returned. I told him the whole story. He said the alligator was so heavy that he broke something underneath the accelerator. It wasn't expensive; John made the repairs. John said he still tells the story to this day, because it's the first time he ever had to repair a vehicle because of an alligator.

I'll bet this is the first time any of you have ever heard of an alligator trying to steal a car!

Snowbound

This is a quick story that involved a very unusual rescue. It was Thanksgiving, 2009. I was at my sister's house celebrating with my family. Detroit had just been hit with over two feet of snow, and I received a phone call from the Northville Township Police Department. The Sergeant wanted to know if I could come out there and identify a snake. They had no idea what kind it was, although a few of them thought it was a rattlesnake. I asked where they got it and the Sergeant said they found it in the snow.

I had no idea what to expect when I got there, but I know that snakes don't ever come out in the snow. All snakes that are native to Michigan hibernate in the winter for two reasons. The first is there is no food for them. The second is more important...they are poikilothermic, which means they can't regulate their own body temperature and they would literally freeze to death.

I drove to Northville with my family, which took forever because of the horrible road conditions. This is the same police department that had called me to rescue Beefy-T Bad Boy, the large alligator I referred to earlier in this book. They met me in their parking lot and brought me into their dispatch office, where I noticed a 55-gallon barrel sitting upright on the floor. It was completely duck-taped closed, while there were several weights placed on top, as well. The officers made damn sure that whatever was in that barrel wasn't getting out!

I said, "Let me guess…it's in there."

All four officers said, "Yes." They all got up and moved to the other side of the room, as I took the weights off and started unraveling the tape. I carefully lifted the top and peered in, not knowing what to expect.

I immediately knew what it was and stated, "Yep, it's definitely a rattlesnake." I reached in, nonchalantly picked it up, and brought it out. All four of these officers freaked out, and I had no choice but to tell them I was joking.

It was one of the largest Eastern milk snakes I had ever seen…a little over four-feet in length. They are native to Michigan and completely harmless. Here's the weird thing…I asked where they obtained this snake. One of the officers said an old man and his wife, who lived in a farm house not far from the police station, had found it in their yard. They had just arrived home and parked their car in the driveway. They hadn't shoveled the snow yet, and they spotted the snake on top of the snow in their yard.

There were no footprints around the snake, so nobody could have placed it there. It definitely didn't crawl there through the snow on its own. To this day, no one can figure out how this snake arrived where it did. I hypothesized that a bird might have carried it and somehow dropped it, but where would a bird have found it? One of the officers thought it had escaped from someone's house, but it couldn't have crawled to this man's yard.   If anyone reading this has any ideas how this snake ended up in the snow, please let me know.   The snake was miraculously alive when I arrived at the police station, and it lived with us for another two years before dying of old age.

Going Up

Me & Tinker at a school in 2007

This is a pretty funny story that happened while I was performing one of my "Creatures of The Night" shows back in 2002. I have an actual hearse that's customized with all kinds of spooky animal decals on it which I use to transport my animals and tricks for Halloween performances. I only use this hearse during the month of October, and people book Animal Magic way in advance for these shows. I bring out animals people usually associate with Halloween: Bats, snakes, tarantulas, scorpions, etc.

I'm known for my big dogs, and Tinker, our 200-pound Great Dane, was with me this day. I was performing a couple of shows at the Ann Arbor Hands-On Museum. Tinker was dressed up in his skeleton costume; an adult XL costume usually fits our Danes. We arrived in my hearse!

We went in and found out that I would be performing in the basement, where this museum had enough room to accommodate large crowds. It was just Tinker, my other animals and me. I finished setting up and eventually started my first show. It was standing-room only, and everything went according to plan. Once I had finished the show, I let everyone know that they could come up and pet Tinker.

People approached me with questions and wanted autographs, so I started to accommodate them. I looked up about ten minutes later to see a woman entering the room holding Tinker by the collar. I asked why she was holding him and explained that he was friendly and would never hurt anyone. She said Tinker was on the elevator; I asked what she meant.

She stated that she had never seen anything funnier. She watched Tinker walk into the hall and wait in front of the elevator doors until they opened. Tinker walked into the elevator and traveled up to the lobby, where he exited and walked around. He then waited for the doors to reopen and got back in. Tinker rode it back down to the basement, where I was. He then repeated this over and over, while this lady watched.

I was too busy answering questions and signing autographs to even notice he was missing. I'm so used to him staying right by me that I never thought he would go joyriding. This lady told me that she watched

Tinker ride the elevator up and down five times! She rode the elevator a couple of times to see what he was doing and eventually got worried that he might leave the lobby, which is when she grabbed his collar and brought him back to me.

Tinker passed away in 2009. He slept in my daughter's bed every night of his life, and we still miss him to this day.

Tinker Time

Tinker relaxing outside in 2008

Here is a copy of Tinker's obituary that we put in a couple of our local papers, as well as, on our web site. Tinker was extremely well-known throughout the United States. We wanted to let everyone know he was gone, but not forgotten:

Tinker Was Majestic Until the End

I have some sad news to pass along this month. We had to put Tinker, our beloved 204-pound "Gentle Giant" to sleep today, October 27, due to bone cancer. He lived a long, happy life and touched many peoples' lives. As close as we can figure, over 600,000 people had pet him in his almost nine years with us. He accompanied me to most of my performances and was well-known and loved by all. He slept in my daughter's bed almost every night since he was born on February 12, 2000. He was one of the best friends anyone could ever have.

This was a hard decision for us to make, but we believe it was the correct one. None of us would ever allow an animal to suffer just for our benefit. Tinker's cancer spread rather quickly the past two months. He was still in good spirits until the very end, and he even tried to play soccer with me yesterday, even though he could barely walk. He held his head high and never showed any pain. He will be missed tremendously.

I would like to add a couple of "Tinker stories" to this letter. The first was the time Tinker decided to play with a skunk before realizing just what it was! I had to give him a tomato juice bath at midnight in Houghton Lake. We both froze, and we both stunk for weeks!

The other story happened when I was performing at the Ann Arbor Hands-On Museum a few years ago. One minute Tinker was in the basement with me, and the next minute a patron brought him back into the room where I was. She explained that she saw Tinker get on the elevator and ride it up to the main floor to search for handouts in the kitchen. Tinker never ceased to amaze us with his intelligence and his unique ability to locate food.

I always asked the children at my shows what their favorite animal was, and almost all of them would respond, "Tinker." This always amazed me because I had just shown them many rare and amazing animals such as a sloth, various primates, large macaws and cockatoos, honey bears, a kangaroo, and they still said Tinker was their favorite.

He accompanied us every Halloween in full costume, and even let us dress him up in the most ridiculous outfits. He never fussed about anything. Many of you remember Merlin, Tinker's 238-pound dad, from the many appearances he made. We have peace knowing Tinker and Merlin are both back together again. Please feel free to send us your stories or memories regarding Tinker. We would love to see them, and it would help in our healing process.

Thanks again for all your support through his very rough time. I hate when an animal needs to be euthanized, but every living thing must come to an end. It's much better to focus on all the good times and fun things, rather than on their final days.

One last note, here is what Tinker ate his final morning:

Two bagels

A full box of Lorna Doone cookies

Eight White Castle hamburgers

Two scoops of vanilla custard from Culver's

Like I stated earlier, Tinker LOVED to eat!

Pistol Packing Python

I received a phone call about six years ago from a lady in Detroit who had just moved into a house. She said there was a large snake in her home, and she wanted to know if I would come out and trap it. I asked where it was; she told me she had no clue. I asked her how she knew there was a snake. She told me she saw it near the wash tub when she went downstairs to wash clothes. She screamed and ran upstairs before calling me. I asked if it was still there, so I stayed on the phone while she checked. She got back on the phone after a few minutes and told me it was gone.

I informed her that the snake was probably still in her house, but I would have to charge her for driving out there to search for it. I explained I couldn't drive all the way to her house for free. She was in a really bad neighborhood in Detroit, and I didn't want to pay for gas. Also, it would take at least a few hours, but I told her that I would do it. She said she would call me back when she had some money.

I heard from her again a few days later. She said she spotted it that morning, but it was now gone. I asked her to describe it; she said it was really big. I told her again that I would have to charge her. She repeated she would get back to me when she had some money. That was the last time I heard from her.

I received a phone call from the news room at Channel 2, Fox News, about two weeks later. They wanted to know if I would meet one of their film crews at a house in Detroit. They had received a call regarding a loose snake in someone's house. I didn't put two and two together yet, because I receive a lot of calls like this. I never charge police or TV shows for my services, so I checked my schedule to make sure I had the time. I told them I could meet them at the house. I let them know it might take me awhile to find the snake, and there was a chance I wouldn't be able to find it at all. I said I would try to do my best.

They gave me the address, so I started to drive to this house. I realized it was located in the very worst area of Detroit. I really couldn't believe people actually lived in these run-down houses. Most of them were either fire-bombed or boarded up.

I saw Fox 2's van and pulled up behind them. They were waiting for me to arrive before entering the house. I got out and saw Aundrea Isom exit the van. I was relieved to see a familiar face, because I had worked with her before on a couple of stories. I also remembered she was deathly afraid of arachnids and snakes. I couldn't believe they sent her to cover this story! She came over and gave me a hug and told me she was glad I was there. I said, "Let's go find this snake." We proceeded up the steps to the front door.

Andrea and the cameraman had me go first. I knocked on the door. The lady of the house opened the door to meet us, and we all took a step back. There were two very large pit bulls trying to get us through the door. These dogs were not trying to make nice… they really wanted to tear us apart! The lady told us to hang on while she put her dogs away. She returned a couple minutes later.

She asked if I was the one she had been calling, and then it dawned on me…this was the same lady who had been calling me about a snake and didn't have the money for me to come out there. She then called the Problem Solvers at Channel 2; they, in turn, called me. I told her that I was the same guy. Since I was already there, I would try to find this "giant" snake.

We entered the house and were led downstairs to the basement, where this lady showed me the laundry tub where she had last spotted the snake. Andrea was hiding behind the cameraman, who was far behind me, just in case I found it. The cameraman wasn't too scared; he filmed everything. I looked all around the laundry tub, on the floor, at the pipes near the ceiling, and I didn't see a trace of any snake.

I heard a scratching noise coming from inside one of her closets. I knew that snakes don't have paws or claws. I went to open the door and the lady yelled, "Don't open the door," right as I opened it. A pit bull puppy came running out of the closet. I have no idea why she was hiding it from us, and I didn't really care. I just wanted to find this snake and get out of there. I was really worried about my van that was parked in front of the house.

The lady took the puppy upstairs, while I kept searching for the snake. I located a snake skin hanging from one of the pipes near the ceiling. I found a bucket to stand on to retrieve the shed skin. It was about four-feet long and had been recently shed. It looked to be from a ball python or a boa constrictor. I couldn't really tell. At least, now I had proof there was a snake!

This house had a drop ceiling. I told the cameraman that I was going to lift up the ceiling panels and peer in with a flashlight to see what I could find. By this time, the lady had come back downstairs; I asked if she had a ladder. She found a small step ladder, and I said I would make it work.

While I was lifting up the panels, Andrea slowly came over to me to ask what I was doing. I decided it was time to mess with her. Remember, the cameraman was filming all of this. Andrea asked if I was worried about being bitten, and I told her no, because the odds of it being a venomous snake were pretty slim. I knew from the snake skin that it wasn't venomous, but there was a slim possibility there might be other snakes loose in this house. I told Andrea it would be good television if it bit me, but that it wouldn't do much damage…I would just bleed. I also told her it would be easier for me to retrieve the snake if it bit me and wrapped around my hand. I compared it to fishing, using my hand as bait.

Andrea laughed as I reached up into the ceiling. Without looking, I pretended to pull out a snake. You can probably still find this story on line somewhere. I **screa**med, causing Andrea to drop the microphone, shout, swear (which they edited out of the tape) and run halfway up the stairs. The cameraman knew I was playing around and kept the tape rolling. I never yell when I get bitten…that doesn't accomplish anything. I only yelled to scare Andrea, which apparently worked.

The cameraman started laughing and Andrea eventually crept back down the stairs near us. She hit me, playfully, in the arm, and I told her I would keep looking for the real snake. One-half of the basement was much lower than the other. In fact, I could reach the ceiling without using a ladder on this side. I started pushing up the panels and something happened that hadn't even crossed my mind. It should have occurred to me, especially in this type of neighborhood.

I pushed up the first panel and this heavy black thing fell out from the ceiling and hit me on my right foot. It was a loaded 38-revolver. It could easily have fired when it hit my foot, or my hand could have hit the trigger when I was reaching into the ceiling.. A number of things could have happened and any one of us could have been wounded or even killed.

The tenant said the gun wasn't hers and told us the former tenants were drug dealers. We then assumed there were other guns throughout the house. I decided to be extra careful from then on. I didn't find any other guns in that section of the basement, so I directed my attention to the higher area. I got back on the ladder and focused above the laundry tub. I moved one of the ceiling tiles witnessing a snake's tail slithering away. I got my flashlight, focused it in the direction of where the snake was going and saw it coil around one of the pipes. It was an adult ball python, which I knew was completely harmless.

I reached in and grabbed it, knowing the worst it could do was bite me, and I proceeded to unwind it from the pipe. I guessed the drug dealers kept it in the house as a pet. It must have somehow escaped before they left. Ball pythons are native to Africa and can't survive Michigan winters, so I knew it didn't crawl into the house.

To me, the weirdest part of this story wasn't the snake in the ceiling…it was the loaded gun that fell from the ceiling onto my foot!

Celebrity Surprise 21st

Hayden Panettiere & Widget

Neve Campbell   Wes Craven

Hayden's Birthday Cake

I received a phone call from a booking agent while I was on vacation in July of 2010. Lauren wanted to know if I was available on August 21st for a celebrity event. I asked who the celebrity was and Lauren told me she didn't know. It was all hush-hush. I knew I was already booked to perform five shows at the Sumner Daze Festival, where I perform every year. I told Lauren I could try to reschedule my previous commitment when I returned to my office in a few days.

Lauren told me the event would be at a nightclub somewhere around the Ann Arbor area, but that's all she knew at the time. When I returned home, I called Carlene, who is in charge of the Sumner Daze Festival. I asked if we could adjust my performance times and explained why. I said I would really like to do this celebrity event, but I was committed to them first and would abide by her decision.. As it was, I had a three-hour drive each way to this festival, and I wanted to leave there early enough to get back to my sanctuary, put my animals away, repack and then drive to this other event.

Carlene is super sweet and told me to just perform four shows and omit the five o'clock performance. It was just going to be for her employees anyway. This way, I would be done at two o'clock, and I might be able to make it back in time. She said the only other stipulation was to tell her who the celebrity was. I told her I honestly didn't know, but I would call her when I found out.

I called Lauren back; she told me she still didn't have much information, but I was to meet her the following week at The Cavern Club in Ann Arbor. She said there was going to be a meeting to discuss everything. Everyone I knew was trying to figure out for whom this event was going to be. We were guessing who was going to be in town, whose birthday was on that date and what movies were being filmed in Detroit.

I arrived at The Cavern Club the following week. A man came up to me, who I immediately recognized as David Arquette. He shook my hand and introduced himself. Not wanting to be a jerk and saying, "I know who you are," I just shook his hand and said, "Hi, my name is Mark and I'm with Animal Magic." Lauren, the lady who had originally called me, was also there, as was Jeff Beecher, who owns Beecher's Madhouse in Las Vegas. He's a big name and very well-known. He's also not a nice man to work with, as he's very mean, abrasive and puts everyone down. He doesn't ask people to do things…he tells them, and they better do what he says or they are gone.

David Arquette was the complete opposite, being extremely pleasant and easy to work with. I talked to David, and he then talked to Jeff about what they wanted to do with this party. It was at this point that I found out whose birthday it was. They were throwing a Surprise 21st Birthday Party for Hayden Panettiere. Hayden is very well-known, because she's been acting since she was a child. She starred in "Fern Gully," "I Love You Beth Cooper," "Heroes," where she was the cheerleader, as well as, many other feature films. The cast of "Scream 4" was staying in a mansion in Ann Arbor where they were filming. David wanted to throw Hayden a Surprise 21st Birthday Party, because they were working on this movie together, and he's a really nice guy.

Jeff Beecher is a personal friend of David's, as well as his business partner. Jeff's also in the entertainment business, owning a few nightclubs in Hollywood and Las Vegas. David and Jeff wanted to know if I could supply some animals for the party, because Hayden is an avid animal lover. Hayden supports many rescues and her favorite animals are dolphins, monkeys and goats. Yes, you read that right…goats!

Here is how they wanted the party to work. The Cavern Club is a large, three-level nightclub. They wanted each floor to have a different theme. The plan was to bring Hayden in on the first level for dinner. Next, they were going to walk her up to the second level, where they wanted me to greet her with a giant snake. I explained that wasn't the best of ideas, because it's not plausible to stand there for that long with a giant snake wrapped around me. David then asked if I could bring a giant snake and wrap it around Hayden. I said, "No," for obvious reasons.

68

David then switched gears and wanted to know if I could have one of my macaws perched where people could come by and get their pictures taken. I explained that wouldn't work either, because they were planning on having a band on each level and the loud music would make any bird uncomfortable. Also, I knew that people were going to be drinking. I didn't want anyone messing with my animals, especially a macaw with a beak powerful enough to severe a finger in an instant. I told David that it wouldn't work, and he agreed.

David then wanted to know if I had a monkey and a goat. He wanted me to bring out a monkey and let Hayden hold it and get her picture taken. Then, after Hayden had a chance, other guests could do the same. I said that would be no problem because I had Widget, the largest, most endangered lemur on Earth. Widget was a member of our family and lived in our house. She ate whatever we had for dinner. I raised her since she was a baby and trusted her with anyone. I also told David I had a goat that was easy with which to work. In reality, I had no goat, nor did I know of anyone who had one. I figured it would be easy to locate, and I wanted this gig.

After talking for awhile, David said he had to get back to the set. Jeff was extremely polite, up until David left. Then the real Jeff took over. He was known for throwing very elaborate, inappropriate Hollywood parties. I'm now thinking I want nothing to do with this party. It's not worth endangering my employees or my animals.

We finally walked up to the third floor, where David had said he wanted me with my animals. I'll explain that in a minute. Jeff sat down with Lauren and I couldn't believe how he talked down to her. He was talking down to everyone there. David Arquette was paying for the party, but Jeff was pretty much in charge of setting it up. Jeff wanted the party to be a circus-like atmosphere. He wanted stilt-walkers, jugglers, acrobats, animals, fire-eaters, and dwarfs. In fact, Lauren had a man and a woman show up who did an aerial acrobatics performance with fire. This female performer was extremely good-looking. They came to audition for Jeff and performed really well. Keep in mind, these were professional acrobats. She and her partner did the most amazing stunts. He was hanging from the ceiling and lifting her up, while she was twirling fire. They were amazing! Jeff called Lauren over and said, right in front of this woman, "Don't you have anybody who is better looking and skinnier?"

Now, the female acrobat heard this, and not that it would have mattered, but she was an extremely attractive woman. She was a professional acrobat who was really good at what she did. Well, they walked out, and Lauren was devastated because the woman was actually a friend of hers. Jeff was cutting everybody down, except me. He knew he had no choice, because I was the only one who could provide the animals around here that he needed.

Jeff then called me over and told me what he really wanted. I was appalled at what he said, but not too surprised. He said he was flying in a bunch of midgets and dwarfs from California, and he wanted me to have a diaper on the goat. He would then have one of the midgets lead the goat around the bar on a leash. He thought it would look funny. I would never stress out my animals, scare them, or place them in any danger, and I was very worried about this party because of Jeff Beecher's reputation. I was debating if I still wanted to do this party. I decided that I love Hayden Panettiere and David Arquette , so I would go through with it…I would just do it on MY terms.

I told Jeff I wasn't comfortable with anyone, other than my employees and me, handling any of my animals. I told him I wouldn't permit anyone to walk the goat anywhere. Keep in mind that I didn't own a goat and had no idea where to find one. I told him I would use one of my photographers, not his. I was thinking my wife would love to attend this secret celebrity-filled party, and I could get her in under the guise of being my photographer. I knew that this opportunity to be around all of these big celebrities might never happen again, especially not in Michigan. I could see if I was based in California or New York, but not in here Michigan.

My wife has done this at other events, where she would take the photos and we would print them while people waited. It was a way to generate additional money for our rescue. We had a state-of-the-art printer, and it printed pretty quickly. I told Jeff my photographer would take everyone's photo as they came over to meet Widget, our lemur. I explained I needed a roped-off area from where we could work. I told him the corner where the pool table was would work perfectly. We could be behind it and set up our printer on the table. We could place the photos on the table, and the guests could pick them up at their convenience. Jeff loved that idea, so we were all set.

There was still the problem of finding a tame goat with less than a month to go until party time. I decided to purchase a baby goat that was still on the bottle, and work with it. My logic was that I would have one of my employees hold the goat as people walked in. There was no way I was letting Jeff have one of his midgets walk it around. I made some calls, while driving home, and found a friend of a friend who raised goats. I obtained his number and called him. He told me he didn't have any babies, but he did have a very friendly adult goat that I could borrow, as long as I would be held responsible, if anything went wrong. I guaranteed him nothing would happen to his goat. In fact, I told him he would probably have the only goat in the world with a bodyguard. He agreed to this, so I told him I would pick the goat up the day before the event.

The first call I made when I arrived home was to Russ, one of my nephews, who works with me from time to time. He was a bouncer at a nightclub in Lansing. He knows what he's doing, and I knew he would jump at the chance to work at this party. I figured I would bring Russ as the goat's personal bodyguard. His only job would be to protect this goat. He (Russ, not the goat) jumped at the chance. I figured I was ready.

All the original people hired for this event either backed out or got fired by Jeff. Lauren, the agent who originally called me, quit after Jeff made her cry so many times that she finally decided it just wasn't worth it. Everybody that I had met earlier was gone. I was the lone remaining one, because Jeff had no choice if he wanted the animals, and he knew not to upset me. He was also known for not paying people and making numerous court appearances. I had him pay me in advance.

I called him a couple of weeks before the party and gave him my price, to which he agreed. I called him back after Lauren told me she had quit. I said I needed to be paid up front or I wasn't doing it. He said, "No problem, no problem." He told me to come in on Monday, and he would pay me. I arrived at the agreed-upon time; Jeff was nowhere to be found.

Here's what I observed when I walked in: There was a lady inside the door surrounded by six midgets, five guys and a girl. I recognized one of the guys from a movie and the girl was familiar also, but I couldn't remember from where. They all came up to me and introduced themselves, wanting to know all about the animals. After talking with them for awhile, I asked the lady where Jeff was. She said he called her earlier and told her he wasn't going to be able to make it. I said,

"OK, please call him and tell him that I'm out, and I'm not going to be able to do it." I walked out.

I received a phone call less than an hour later from Jeff, apologizing to me. He said, "Listen, I have your check in my hands right now and I can have it back here, if you want to pick it up tomorrow. We really need you, so please reconsider." I knew he was in a bind, with only a couple days left until the party. There was no possible way for him to find anyone else with a monkey AND a goat on such short notice with the price I gave him. I wasn't making a lot. I was mainly doing this so my wife and I could meet the celebrities.

I drove back the next day where the lady met me at the door, apologized and handed me an envelope containing my check. I could tell Jeff wasn't happy about paying me in advance, but he knew I wasn't bluffing and that I wouldn't show. I called Lauren and let her know I had already been paid; she was shocked. She told me I was the only one who had received any money, besides the owner of the club.

I loaded a large dog crate into my van and drove to this man's house on Friday, August 20, to pick up his goat. Dave told me this goat would do anything for food, so we put some in the crate and the goat walked right in. Dave and I lifted the crate into my van, and I drove him back to our sanctuary. I knew I only had to house him for two nights...that night and the night of the party. I would bring him back to our sanctuary after the party to sleep and return him to his owner the next day.

Well, I'll be the first person to admit that I know almost nothing about farm animals. I mainly deal with exotics, not hoofed stock. I had no idea how strong goats were, but I found out soon enough. I placed this goat in one of our outdoor enclosures, which was constructed of cyclone fencing, the same as most of your backyard fences. It was previously used to house two of my six-foot-long binturongs, the longest prehensile-tailed mammals in the world. I figured if the binturongs couldn't get out, then no little goat would be able to get out. Boy, was I wrong!

Without exaggerating, this goat broke out within one minute of me closing and locking the door! He used his horns as a battering ram and easily broke through the door. This goat had already emerged from the other side of my sanctuary by the time I had turned the corner. I was astounded! I got some food and called him over. I led him back to the cage and put him back in it. I then took eight large chains and wrapped them around the posts and door to make sure he was now secure. I stood there and watched as he finished his food and then battered the door, completely destroying it. I was at a loss as how to keep this goat locked in the cage. The only thing I could think of was to take six, heavy chain-link panels and lean them against the battered door. There was no way anything could push through that much weight. I knew it would be a pain for me to go in and out, but I saw no other way. It worked, and he stayed in there throughout the night.

I awakened at 3:00 a.m., the morning of the party, packed up my animals and headed out for the three-hour drive to Sumner, Michigan. I performed all four shows and left there at 3:00 p.m. I arrived back at my sanctuary a little after 6:00 p.m., where Russ and my wife were waiting. They helped me put the animals back in their cages, as I packed up Widget and the goat. I made sure we had the camera, fresh batteries, the printer and paper. Once we determined we were ready, we took off for Ann Arbor. I let Russ and Diane know what the plan was once we arrived. My main concern was for the animals' safety. I explained to Russ that he was to guard the goat with his life and not let anyone near it. Diane's job was to oversee everything while taking the photos. I was to hold Widget, which actually served two purposes: I would make sure she was under control, and of course, I would have to be in all the photos!

We arrived and noticed that the Cavern Club seemed empty. I pulled up right in front of the alley to make it easier to bring the animals in on our dolly. I was told to arrive at seven and set up because Hayden was arriving at 8:00 p.m. for dinner. They didn't want her suspecting anything. Jeff Beecher came running out, yelling at me. I had already prepared Russ and my wife for how mean this guy was. I pointed him out and said, "That's Jeff Beecher."

Jeff yelled, "Get out of the way. Move your van. Hurry up. Get out of here."

I was already familiar with this guy by now, but Diane and Russ weren't. They couldn't believe how abrupt he was. He didn't faze me. I calmly told him that I needed to unload the animals before I moved my van. Russ and I loaded the goat's crate and Widget's crate onto the dolly, and Diane drove the van to a nearby parking lot to hide it. For those of you who have never seen my van, it's almost impossible to miss. It's decorated with animals on all four sides and the top. I understand why Jeff didn't want it right in front, but I knew we had all kinds of time, and he could have been polite about it.

Once inside, Jeff laid another bombshell on me. He said the elevator was broken. We would have to use the outside fire escape to bring the animals up to the third level. He left and went back inside to let me figure out what to do. My dolly can't go up stairs; it's on wheels! So, we had no choice other than to lift it and literally carry it all the way up. Diane caught up to us by the time we arrived at the third floor. We banged on the door for someone to let us in; security opened it. The three of us were amazed at how nice everything looked. The decorations were amazing and there was even a life-sized, hand-sculpted cake in the shape of a dolphin that read, "Happy Birthday Hayden."

The area I requested was roped off for us, and the owner came over to introduce himself. He was extremely nice saying, "Whatever you need is yours; just let anyone here know. Don't worry about a thing." What a great guy. We set everything up in the corner, plugged in the printer to warm it up, put fresh batteries in the camera, and made sure Widget's and the goat's cages were clean.

I brought a few diapers with me to protect the club's floors (and the guests' shoes) from goat poop. Those of you who know me know I don't believe in diapering animals. I have never diapered any of my monkeys, bears, or any other animal, because they are not human. I just don't think it's right to humanize animals, but this was for a different reason. I attempted to put one of the diapers on the goat, not thinking in advance how difficult a task this might be. Russ helped me by feeding the goat, while I put the diaper on him...the goat, not Russ! I finally got it on the goat and held it in place with duck tape. The tape wasn't adhering to the goat's fur…it was only sticking to itself. This was one of the silliest sights I have ever seen.

We waited forever, because Hayden's limo was late. The Killer Flamingos, the band that was to play on out level, came over and started talking to us to kill time. It looked like the Secret Service was there, because there were bodyguards at every doorway. The only other people on our level at this time, besides the band, were the bartenders.

One of the workers came up a little past ten o'clock and told everyone Hayden had arrived and was eating downstairs. We started getting excited, even more so when some of the guests starting coming in. I was a huge fan of the first person to approach us. Russ, nor Diane, knew who he was, but I knew it was Wes Craven, one of the most famous horror movie directors in history. He was in town directing, "Scream 4," so it made sense that he was invited. He came over with his long-time girlfriend, when they saw Widget on my shoulder. Wes's girlfriend told me she spent time in Africa and Madagascar and loved animals. She wanted her picture taken with Widget, so I told her and Wes to each get on one side of Widget and me, while Diane snapped their photo.

Next, someone else approached, who I didn't recognize. I planned on only being nice to the celebrities I knew, having no clue who this woman was. She asked if she could get her picture with Widget, and I blew her off. I said, "Not right now. She needs to rest, but feel free to come back later." This lady walked away and Diane came over to me and asked, "Do you know who that was?" I responded, "No, so I got rid of her."

My wife objected, "No, you've actually had a crush on her for years. You were just rude to Neve Campbell!" Neve starred in, "I Know What You Did Last Summer," "Scream 1, 2, 3 & 4," "Wild Things," and too many more to list. I had just blown her off!

Diane did damage control and ran after Neve and apologized for me. Diane told Neve that Widget could pose for a picture now. Diane brought Neve back to us, and I had her stand next to me while I held Widget. Diane took the photo; thankfully, everything worked out all right. That photo is at the beginning of this chapter.

Next, David Arquette came up and talked to me for awhile, as did many other people. The only celebrity who was too big for his britches was Matthew Lillard. He was rude to every "non-celebrity" and just shot pool on the next table for as long as we were there.

Hayden hadn't arrived to our level yet, but someone shouted that she was coming up the stairs. Hayden was now aware of the party, after seeing the second floor, but had no clue what was on our level. We got the animals ready. I had Widget on my shoulder, Russ had the goat's leash and Diane had the camera ready. Hayden walked in and all eyes fell upon her. She was more gorgeous in person and extremely friendly. She started walking along the side of the pool tables, and you could see her eyes light up when she saw the goat. Goats are one her favorite animals and she made a beeline for Russ, who was in the corner holding the goat's leash. Hayden, and whoever was with her, who we believe was either her publicist or her best friend, asked if she could pet the goat. Keep in mind that Hayden was dressed to the nines in a gorgeous, and presumably very expensive, gown. I told her it was her party, and of course she could pet the goat.

She knelt on the floor in front of the goat and started petting him. Hayden was in heaven, and it was really cool to observe. I had been so worried about this party and what might happen, never expecting Hayden to be so friendly. I heard some pretty bad rumors about Hayden…that she wasn't really an animal lover at all and that it was all just a publicity act. This couldn't be further from the truth; she was awesome! After a couple minutes of petting the goat, she looked up and noticed Widget. She stood up and asked us to put the goat back in his carrier, so he wouldn't get too stressed out. I told her that Beecher wanted us to walk the goat around for everyone to see and she said, "No way! This is my party and I'm telling you it's ok to put him away." I was so relieved to hear her say that, so I gave Russ the ok to put the goat back. Hayden then said we could take the goat back to our vehicle, so as not to stress it with the loud music that was going to be playing later on. I told her it was safer for the goat to remain with us than to be in a van by himself.

Hayden then asked if she could hold Widget. I said, "Of course," as I handed Widget over to her, with Diane taking a bunch of photos. After a few minutes, the coolest thing happened. Hayden asked me the following, "Can we go somewhere private, so I can play with this magnificent creature?"

I was thinking, "Wow, people flew in from all over the country for Hayden's party, and she wants to spend it with us!" Paris Hilton, Courtney Cox, Neve Campbell, Emma Roberts, Hayden's family, and the list went on and on. I knew Hayden didn't plan to spend the evening with us…she just wanted some time with Widget.

I called David Arquette over and asked if there was an enclosed room where we could take Hayden and let Widget run loose. He told us to wait there for a second and that he would be right back. He returned a short time later telling us to follow him. He said he was taking us to the room where they had dinner. We followed David down two flights of stairs to this large banquet room. Russ wasn't happy, because he had to stay on the third level with the goat and our printer. I didn't want to make him wait in the van, so I figured it would be better for him to stay up there.

My wife brought the camera while I carried Widget. David went back to the party right after showing us to the room. We were in this room with Hayden, her mom and brother, her publicist, one of Hayden's best friends and Hayden's bodyguard. That was it, just the eight of us. Hayden's publicist asked us if we would forgo any photographs. She said Hayden just wanted to spend time with Widget. Diane put the camera down, and we all sat at this humongous table. Hayden was sitting next to me, as Widget was climbing all over her. Leslie (Hayden's mom) came over and held Widget, as did Jayden (Hayden's brother). Hayden loved playing with Widget so much that time stood still.

David Arquette came down looking for Hayden 45 minutes later. Keep in mind that this whole party was for Hayden, and she was nowhere to be found, because she had just spent the last 45 minutes downstairs in a room with us!

David told Hayden that she had to get upstairs, because they wanted her to cut her birthday cake. Hayden looked at us and said we could take our animals home now. I told her Beecher wanted us to stay there until 2:00 a.m.; it wasn't even midnight yet. She said, "It's MY party, and I love these animals. Thank you so much for bringing them. Take them home…you did a great job. I really appreciate this, and it's a great birthday." Hayden hugged my wife and me before she headed upstairs. We had no way to get through the massive crowd, because I had Widget's large carrier. There were people all over the stairwell; it was a crazy scene!

All of a sudden, who comes to our rescue? David Arquette, who said, "Mark, come here. I'm going to lead the way…follow me." He started yelling, "Coming through…monkey coming through. Let's go everybody, move it," as he was telling Diane and me to just follow him. He led us back up to the third level, where he went left, while we went right. We arrived back to Russ, who wasn't real happy, because he loves Hayden and would have given anything to be down there with us. He only got to meet her for a few minutes, but at least he has a picture with her to remember the night.

Many of Hayden's guests invited us to stick around for the rest of the party, but I didn't want to stress out the animals, especially when we heard about the private fireworks that were scheduled to go off within the next 30 minutes. The band started playing, and everyone was dancing. We waited until Hayden got on stage to make a speech before we decided to leave. It was time for us to go, so we packed everything up. Security told us to go ahead and use the Emergency Exit before the fireworks started. They opened the door for us. Russ and I had to carry the dolly back down the stairs; we eventually made it back to terra firma. We had a great night…we met a lot of celebrities, everyone was nice (except Jeff Beecher and Matthew Lillard), and the animals did fine.

All in all, it couldn't have gone any better!

A.J.

I am only able to get away with my family a couple times a year because of my career. I work seven days a week, every day of the year, except for six days in July and six days in August. I take my family to Houghton Lake during these days.

Every July, for the past 19 years, the same family stays in the cabin by ours. We've know Andrew, this family's son, since he was born. Even though we only got to see him one week out of the year, we still knew him pretty well. In 1999, when he was seven-years old, he had some severe medical problems. I believe he had multiple seizures and strokes, which caused him to walk with a limp and have limited use of his left arm. A.J., as we knew him, never complained about anything, and he would always come over to greet us when we arrived. He was always so nice to our dogs. In fact, I remember one year we had a birthday party for Zeus, one of our Great Danes, and A.J. wore a party hat and joined in the celebration.

A.J. loved to play Carpet Ball, a game that he played almost daily at Houghton Lake with my dad. He also liked to play Rummy Cube. A.J. was always smiling, with this day being no different. My wife and I would comment every year that we couldn't wait to see A.J. in July. We knew everyone at the resort, because the same people kept coming back every year.

There was something special about A.J. that touched everyone he met. A.J. was nowhere to be found when we arrived on July 17th. We were told he had suffered a massive stroke and a grand mal seizure on July 10th, one week before he was supposed to go to Houghton Lake. He was in a coma in a hospital back home. It was a shame, because A.J. told his family that the highlight of his year was going to Houghton Lake.

A.J.'s sister, Katy, would post a blog almost daily about his condition which kept worsening. The doctors induced a coma, because all the seizures were destroying A.J.'s brain. He would start seizing every time they thought he was well enough to come out of the coma. It was awful; we thought about him daily. A.J.'s mom and step-dad were with him, but some of his aunts, uncles and grandparents were with us. We would receive updates whenever his family had any.

On July 22nd, A.J.'s family had a meeting and decided to pull the plug to end his suffering. He wasn't getting any better. The doctors went over all of his charts saying that even if he pulled through, he would be blind and wouldn't be able to eat on his own. He passed away peacefully the following morning.

A.J. loved going to my shows and would always be so proud. At his funeral, his mom told me he was so proud of me. He would tell all of his friends about my shows and me. He would tell everyone he got special privileges when he arrived to one of my shows, even though we were filled to capacity. He was allowed early access and always sat in the front row. I remember one show in Westland where I let his family and him in early. A.J. sat dead center in the front row. I brought him up to be my assistant for a magic trick. I let the crowd know he was a personal friend of mine, and I had known him his entire life. His mom told me he was so proud.

Something supernatural happened on July 26, 2012, which is the reason for this story. We went to A.J.'s funeral that day. It was very hard to see this remarkable 19-year-old laying there. I didn't want to remember him like that...he was always so energetic and happy. He had a nonstop smile that was infectious. My parents met us there, and we all went back to our house afterward. I was in the kitchen and Diane was in the living room. Something told me to look out the window, where I saw a mallard duck in our pool. I've lived in this house for nineteen years and have never seen any ducks. Wild ducks don't normally go in someone's pool, because the chlorine isn't palatable. Also, we are surrounded by lakes. A swimming pool would be the last choice for a duck.

I thought I was imaging things when I called Diane out to verify I wasn't crazy. I told her there was a duck in our pool, and she thought I was joking, because I'm always pulling pranks. She said she didn't believe me, but my mom was in the kitchen and verified there was a duck in our pool.

We all went outside and witnessed this duck swimming in our pool. It didn't try to fly away and didn't seem scared. Diane and I grabbed nets and stood on opposite ends of the pool, while my parents and Jamie stood on the sides. I didn't know if this duck was injured or not. I caught it and picked him up with the net to look him over. I couldn't find anything wrong with him. The wings were fine; he seemed healthy. I guessed him to be about three or four-months-old. It was weird because his primary feathers had come in, but his secondary feathers hadn't. This bird wasn't capable of flying yet…it's wings weren't developed enough.

How did it get in our pool? We have a fence around our pool to make sure kids can't fall in. We know the duck couldn't have walked through the fence, and it couldn't have flown over the fence. The duck wasn't there when we got home, because we would have noticed it, as we have to walk by the pool to get into our house. No one came by and put it in the pool after we got home, because our dogs would have alcrtcd us. Wc had no cluc how it got there! We still have it now, because it has never been able to fly.

We named this duck A.J. after Andrew, and I believe this duck was A.J.'s way of telling us he is all right, wherever he is. This duck is unusually friendly and would never hurt anybody, just like A.J.

Rest in Peace Andrew; we miss you.

Mail Order Mamba

I received a phone call from Channel 2 back in 1993. It wasn't called Fox 2 back then, just Channel 2. I was pretty well-known and respected around the country, mainly because I was one of the largest reptile importers. I was successfully breeding reptiles that had rarely been bred in captivity. Channel 2 wanted to know if I would help them with a segment they had in mind. They wanted to show their viewers that anyone could order a deadly animal with just one phone call. This was way before the internet. I agreed to help them, as long as they didn't show my face or identify who I was, because I didn't want any repercussions from their exposure. I had no problem with what they were going to do. I don't think people should be allowed to keep venomous animals as pets. I believe you need to be trained and have proper permits for them, as well as, having no children or other pets in the house.

Here was their plan. Channel 2 had obtained a pricelist in the mail from a reptile dealer in Florida. This place had a reputation for shipping pretty much anything to anyone, as long as they had the money. Channel 2 told me I could order anything off this guy's pricelist that was priced $500 or less; they would pay for it. I was going to be allowed to keep the animal once they were done filming, because they definitely didn't want it! Channel 2 wanted to film everything, from the animal arriving at Detroit Metropolitan Airport to me removing it from the shipping container.

They also wanted to record my phone call when I placed the order.

I remember calling the company and asking the receptionist for a green mamba. For those of you who don't know, the black mamba is the fastest, venomous snake in the world, with the green mamba coming in a close second. Their bite is 100% fatal without anti-venom!

The lady asked where I lived. I told her I'm in Detroit, and the snake could be shipped to DTW, the code for Detroit Metropolitan Airport. She never once asked my age, if I had any experience, or why I wanted a green mamba. She didn't ask if I had a license, and she didn't ask how I would be housing the snake. She needed a credit card, so I used the one provided to me by Channel 2. I gave her all the pertinent information; she ran it through. Everything was fine, and she said they would ship the green mamba in a few days. Channel 2 recorded the whole conversation saying they wanted their film crew to accompany me to the airport when the snake arrived.

I've been shipping reptiles for almost 35 years, and I know the safest ways to do it. Airlines require all venomous animals to be shipped in a pillowcase, which is inside an insulated Styrofoam box, which is inside a wooden crate that is at least ¼ inch thick and screwed closed. It must be clearly labeled: "Live Venomous Reptiles" on at least four sides, with arrows pointing which way is up. There have to be air holes drilled into the wood that are small enough to prevent a finger from going through the crate.

I called Channel 2 when I got the flight information, and they met me at my building before I was to leave for the airport. They accompanied me to the airport, where I signed for the crate. The cargo workers brought the crate to me. I noticed immediately that it was labeled correctly and constructed of ¼ inch wood. I placed the crate in the back of my van and headed to my warehouse, where I then brought it.

My warehouse was located in Westland, which was pretty close to the airport. I drove to the airport three to ten times daily. I placed the crate in one of my "lizard" rooms, because there was a large window connecting it to my office. The TV crew could see through this window and film, while not endangering themselves if something went wrong.

Channel 2 set up their equipment and waited to film, as I proceeded to unscrew the top. I had two of my employees on the far side of the room, just in case I was bitten. I have no fear, which could either help or hinder what I do. I believe that being overly cautious causes you to hesitate and increases your risk of getting bitten. I felt badly for the cameraman, because I didn't have a cordless screwdriver, so he had to wait for me to unscrew over 30 screws by hand! Once only a few screws remained, the cameraman told me they were filming. They wanted to film what would happen when

I lifted the lid. We had no clue if the snake was packed properly. For my sake, I was hoping it was, so it didn't just fly out of the box when I lifted the top.

I carefully lifted the top and saw a Styrofoam box. It was also labeled, "Live Venomous Reptiles." I never wore gloves when handling venomous snakes, because they inhibit my dexterity and I can't feel what I'm doing. I wouldn't want to grab an animal too tightly, causing it injury. By the same token, I wouldn't want to grab an animal too loosely, causing injury to myself. I had a snake hook next to me as I lifted out the Styrofoam box. I removed the tape that was holding it shut. As I removed the lid to this box, I peered in and saw a white pillow case moving around incredibly fast. This pillow case was tied at the top with twine.

I explained what I was doing the whole time, so the cameraman got everything on film. I untied the twine, being extremely careful to keep all of my extremities clear, knowing a snake can easily bite through a pillowcase. The second I got the top untied and carefully opened the bag, a five-foot green mamba came flying out. It came within inches of my left forearm. I grabbed the snake hook, never once taking my eyes off the snake. Hooks are great for boas and pythons, but not for many venomous snakes.

Mambas are very hard to control with a snake hook, because they are so fast and aren't constrictors.

They are arboreal, which means they live in trees and are very agile. Every time I would get the hook under him, he would quickly slither up towards my hand. I finally got him into the aquarium after a few tries, and I securely placed on the locking top. The cameraman was extremely worried during all of this. He told me he was so relieved once I confirmed the snake was secure. Channel 2 left and told me they would call when the story was about to air. It ran a few days later receiving a ton of press. I'm sure you can still find it on line somewhere.

I find it pretty amazing that anyone could order something that deadly right over the phone!

The Vanishing Cobra

My babies hatching

Albinism is a simple recessive gene, which means you breed an albino male to an albino female, and every baby hatched will be albino. I was one of the first people in the United States to successfully breed albino monocled cobras in 1991. I placed all the eggs in one of my incubators and was patiently waiting for them to hatch. I used plastic shoeboxes and a 50/50 mix of vermiculite to water mix for the media. That's what a lot of herpetologists use to incubate reptile eggs. This was way before the high-tech incubators that are available nowadays. I covered about ¾ of each egg with this mixture.

Steve, who was one of my favorite employees, was visiting my house. I started the Reptile Source, my exotic animal wholesale business, back in 1980. I operated it out of my house. That is, until it got too large, not the house...the business! I had animals in every room, including the kitchen and the bathroom. You read that right...every room. I even turned one of the rooms into a cage, which housed two adult binturongs, also called bear cats. Ben and Karia needed this entire 12' x 12' room, because binturongs are the longest, prehensile-tailed mammals in the world. They need a lot of space. These binturongs were six-feet long and had tremendous claws, which were used for climbing.

The basement was used to house two different species of hedgehogs, as well as, two different species of jerboas, which are dwarf kangaroos. I also kept my conures (parakeet), lovebirds and cockatiels down there. Most of my larger parrots (amazons, cockatoos and macaws) were in cages in my living room.

The room across from the binturongs was my snake room, since it was the warmest room. The walls were lined with custom-made melamine snake cabinets, and I placed the shoebox with the cobra eggs in one of the empty ones. I did this for a very good reason…I knew the eggs would hatch in 50-70 days, but I didn't know the exact date. Cobras are extremely venomous. I didn't want them to hatch without me knowing. There was a chance they could escape into the house. These snake cabinets all locked, so the baby cobras wouldn't be able to get out when they pipped their shells.

Steve was visiting when the eggs started hatching. I was ecstatic, because they were the first albino monocled cobras I had ever produced. I don't remember this vividly, but I just talked to Steve this morning, where he now lives in California, and he refreshed my memory, saying he would never forget what happened that morning.

I unlocked the snake cabinet housing the cobra eggs and reached in, all the while telling Steve that cobras can only strike downward. They can't strike like most other snakes, so you're safe as long as you keep your hand above them. One of the newly hatched babies sprang out of the cage right at my face, actually brushing my arm as it flew by me. It landed behind me and slithered across the floor. I told Steve to watch where it went while I checked to see if I had been bitten. By the time I turned around, this baby cobra had already disappeared. I couldn't sleep in the house with a loose cobra, and I couldn't chance it getting out of the house, so Steve and I moved every single cage out of the room. It took all day, but we finally found it hiding behind a large rack of snake cages. I caught it and placed it back in the locked cabinet. Steve and I started moving everything back into the room, which seemed to take forever. We finally finished at 3:00 a.m.

I learned many lessons starting out, and this was one of the most important. Never trust, or turn your back, on any venomous or dangerous animal! I've been very lucky in my career, having actually died only twice and been hospitalized too many times to count. See the story in my first book.

A Slow Death

A friend of mine in Florida, who was an importer, brought in a shipment of giant African land snails back in 1996. These are the largest land snails in the world, obtaining lengths of over one-foot-long! They are amazing and extremely easy for which to care. They literally eat anything. Steve and I actually watched one devour an aluminum Mountain Dew can...the entire can!

They are hermaphrodites, meaning they have both male and female sex organs. They can breed themselves and need no mates. They eventually became outlawed in the United States. They were no longer allowed to be imported, nor were they allowed to be kept as pets. The USDA was worried about the damage they could do to crops if they ever got loose, and rightly so. They wouldn't be able to survive in Michigan, but they could easily survive on the west coast and destroy all the crops...not only crops...they would eat and destroy everything in their paths.

I had just ordered 500 of the snails, before they were banned, and had them shipped to O'Hare Airport in Chicago. I was going to pick them up on my way to the Reptile Expo in Schaumberg, IL. I didn't know the government had already put a cease and desist order on them and had confiscated my entire shipment. Federal agents found out about this shipment and were waiting for us at the airport.

Steve and I arrived, and I was allowed to pick up my shipment. Again, I had no clue these snails were now illegal. Once I signed for them and the agents knew it was me, I was immediately grabbed from the loading dock and handcuffed to a nearby tree. The agents proceeded to open all the crates and told me I was going to jail. I didn't know you could no longer have them in this country, or I never would have brought them in.

The agents took a 55-gallon drum and dumped some of snails into it. They then poured gasoline over them and lit them on fire. I was mortified! They continued until all of them were dead. Steve was in my van this whole time watching. They unlocked my handcuffs. They ended up not arresting me because they realized I had not intentionally done anything wrong. I ordered and paid for these snails way before they banned them, and I hadn't done anything illegal. There was nothing I could do to save the snails. I still feel awful about it to this day.

Once we got back to Michigan, I received a visit from another federal agent who told me I had to give him all the receipts of every giant African land snail I had ever sold. He said the government was going to find them all, confiscate them and destroy them. Again, I had no choice. He watched while I went through all of my records and gave him all the receipts that had the snails on them. The government went to all the pet shops and confiscated every last one of these snails. What they didn't know was Steve had kept a couple at his house and had them for years before they eventually died of old age. They never reproduced for Steve, but he still got years of enjoyment from them.

They are not illegal overseas, and many people have them as pets in Europe. I wish we were also allowed to keep them; they are truly wonderful!

The worst part of the story is these magnificent animals being burned to death, when they could have just been shipped back to Africa. I remember telling the agents, while I was handcuffed, that I would pay for the return shipping, but they wanted no part of it.

The Yellow Stream

Samson   Me & Samson wrestling

If you read my first book, you might recall four stories about Samson, one of my African black-maned lions. Samson was the largest lion in the United States, weighing over 650 pounds as an adult. He would stand on his hind legs and rest his paws on top of his 10-foot tall cage looking down.

I bottle-raised Samson since he was nine days old. I was the only person to ever go in his cage when he matured. I knew how dangerous he was, and I wouldn't be able to live with myself if someone got injured because of my stupidity.

Samson, being a member of the feline family, was extremely playful. He had an eight-foot-long horse trough that was filled with 500 pounds of kitty litter. Samson always used this litter box, except when Steve was there. Samson would wait until Steve's back was turned and then let loose with a deadly accurate stream of urine. It jetted out like a firehouse and would spray wherever Steve was cleaning. It usually doused Steve, who didn't find this very humorous. Steve would always get really mad, and I don't blame him, because Samson constantly urinated on Steve's head. Steve said he would reek from urine for a week, no matter how many showers he took.

I observed Samson doing this quite a few times, and it still remains really funny to me, as it probably does to those of you reading this. I guess it was funny to all, except Steve. He put up with more than any of you could imagine, yet he stayed with me for many, many years until he moved to California. I had completely forgotten about Samson doing this until Steve reminded me this morning on the phone.

Sleuth Seeks Stolen, Slow, Sassy Sloth

I received a phone call around 3:00 p.m. on August 19, 2011 from Beth, a Sumpter Township police officer. I know her quite well. She was one of the responding officers when we were broken into back in 2007. This was the largest story in my first book. These thefts made worldwide news, mainly because animal stories are extremely popular among viewers. We did numerous interviews for quite some time after recovering some of our animals.

I, subsequently, received a phone call from a man who said the sloth we got back was actually his. I told him the sloth was definitely ours. I could identify her by her deformed claw she has on her back right leg. She was born with this deformity; it makes her extremely recognizable. This man saw the story on TV and was sure we had his sloth. He called me numerous times accusing me of stealing his animal. This was back in 2007.

Fast forward to August 19, 2011, when I received the phone call about this story. Beth told me she received a phone call from a man who had seen his sloth on our web site. He accused me of stealing his sloth four years earlier. Beth explained she had to follow up, because it was her job. I told her I understood. She said this guy wanted the police to get his sloth back for him. He said he could prove it was his sloth, because it was micro-chipped. I explained to Beth that I've had this sloth for over ten years, ever since she was eleven-months old, and I would never steal anything from anyone. She told me she had to check our sloth with her microchip scanner to make sure it really was our sloth.

I asked Beth if she was coming out to arrest me, and she told me she knows me well enough to trust that I would bring the sloth to the police station to have it scanned. I replied that I would leave immediately and be there in a few minutes. I placed "Seven" in her carrier and drove over to the police station, where a few officers were waiting for me outside. They all wanted to see this sloth.

I was extremely worried during the short drive, even though I knew for a fact that I had done nothing wrong. You always worry when you are called down to a police station. You hear stories about people being wrongly arrested all the time. Beth had this large paddle-like thing, and she asked me to hold Seven while she scanned her. I held Seven up and she ran this contraption all over my sloth. I asked her where the chip was, and she said she didn't know, but the scanner would pick it up, if there was a microchip.

After thoroughly checking Seven and finding absolutely no trace of any microchip, she told me I was free to go. I left the police station at 5:55 p.m. and headed back to our sanctuary, almost three hours after the initial call. I hope whoever called gets their sloth back, but I really hope I don't keep getting falsely accused…I don't think I can take much more stress.

Jailhouse Rock

This story is the only time I have ever been arrested and thrown in jail for buying and selling endangered tortoises in another state. It's actually the only time I've ever been arrested and thrown in jail...period! Here's what happened:

I've already explained in an earlier chapter about the reptile swaps in Schaumburg, Illinois that I attended every other weekend. I so hated the five-hour drive each way, but I did it every other weekend for over ten years. Steve went with me almost every time, and my girlfriend accompanied us on a few occasions.

This particular Saturday in 1997 started out as all the others. Steve and I packed up the reptiles and headed towards Chicago. I had the most dealer tables at this swap, enough to fill about a quarter of the room. All of our tables were filled with amphibians, turtles and tortoises, snakes, lizards and invertebrates. This particular day was extremely busy, and we didn't have a chance to even take a breath.

Every now and then, someone would come up to our tables and ask me if I wanted to trade for their pet. Their snake had grown too large, their lizard was too much work, etc. I was very easy to deal with and would usually trade in their animal for another one of similar monetary value.

106

A man approached our table and asked Steve if we would purchase his daughter's turtle. Steve came down and asked me to deal with this guy. I was the only one who made the decisions regarding animals. I didn't want to take in a sick or injured animal, and I wanted to make sure the animal we received was worth whatever they were asking for it. The man was holding a box, and he came down to the end where I was standing. He told me he had his daughter's box turtle. His daughter kept it in their backyard and was no longer taking care of it. He wanted to know if I would give him anything for it.

Just a side note...box turtles are not really turtles; they are actually tortoises. The only difference between a turtle and a tortoise is that turtles live in the water and tortoises live on land. That's pretty much it. I had a bin full of Eastern box turtles I was selling for $10 apiece, and without even looking, I told him to place his turtle in with mine and I would give him $6. I never got to see his box turtle, because another man came by less than five minutes later and bought it for $11. I didn't think twice about this at the time.

I couldn't attend the reptile show the next month, because I was invited to a friend's wedding. This was only the second show I missed in over ten years, and as it turns out, I wish I would have attended. I ended up getting arrested because of it. Hang on...I'm getting ahead of myself.

Federal agents showed up at the following swap and issued citations to almost every reptile dealer. These agents had successfully performed a sting operation. It was entrapment, which was legal in Illinois at the time. What they did was thus: The first agent went to a table and traded or sold an ornate box turtle to the dealer. The agents knew how busy the swap was and that no one would notice their endangered ornate box turtle. Everyone just assumed it was an Eastern box turtle, because that's what the agent said he had. Eastern box turtles were abundant and legal to buy and sell, while ornate box turtles, which look extremely similar, were not. I would have known the difference had I taken the time to look, but we were extremely busy. I know that's not an excuse, and I was guilty of doing what everybody else there did.

A few minutes after the first agent traded or sold the ornate box turtle, another agent would follow and purchase the same box turtle within a few minutes. This way they could issue two separate citations…one for purchasing an endangered species and one for selling an endangered species. I found out later they were trying to raise money, and the fines were $100 for each offense.

The problem is I wasn't there when they issued all of these citations, so a bench warrant was issued for my arrest the next time I set foot in Illinois. I had no idea any of this was going on, because I was back here in Michigan.

A couple of weeks later, Steve and I drove back to Illinois for the next swap. We stopped at Chicago's O'Hare Airport to pick up my girlfriend and our daughter, who was only about two-months-old. It was much easier to fly them in than to have them drive with us over five hours in a van filled with reptiles. We picked them up and drove to our usual motel.

I was also bottle-feeding a baby crab-eating macaque (monkey) who needed to be fed every two hours, so he accompanied us to Chicago. We got up the following morning, loaded the animals into the van and headed over to the reptile swap.

We were always the first ones to arrive and get set up. I have a wonderful work ethic, which I learned from my father. We usually arrived by 6:00 a.m., even though the swap didn't open to the public until 10 a.m. This gave us over three hours to set everything up and have a little time left over to relax before everyone came in.

This particular morning, a few of the other vendors came over to me and explained what had happened at the previous show. They told me they received citations a couple weeks earlier, and the federal agents were looking for me. I said I would stay there and wait for the agents to arrive. There was nothing I could do at that point, except pay the tickets.

Little did I know that a bench warrant had been issued for my arrest. Keep in mind…I had this baby monkey to bottle feed, my two-month-old daughter was with me at the swap for the first time, and the place was packed. I was approached by two men about an hour into the swap. One of them said, "Excuse me…we need to talk to you." I had no idea who they were. We were swamped with people buying animals, so I politely asked them to wait a second.

They pulled out their badges and one of them said "We're not asking you…we're telling you! Get out from behind your tables." I told Steve I would be right back, as I crawled under one of my tables. These men told me to follow them outside, where they proceeded to handcuff me. They read me my rights and said they were taking me to jail. I asked what I had done and was told me I had bought and sold endangered animals. They said there was a warrant out for my arrest.

I explained that my two-month-old daughter was inside, and I had a baby monkey that needed his bottle every couple of hours or he would die. I let them know I was the only one who could properly feed him. These agents talked it over and were nice enough to take off my handcuffs and allow me to take my monkey and drive my van to jail. They followed me back in to get the monkey and the cooler with his baby bottles. These agents then had my van sandwiched between their two unmarked cars, so I couldn't get away…like I'm going to go on-the-run because of this! I followed the first car to the Cook County Jail.

We arrived at the police station, where they placed me into a holding cell, along with my baby monkey. There were other prisoners there, but I was placed in solitary. I wasn't allowed a phone call or anything else for that matter. They did warm up my monkey's milk in their microwave, so I could feed him. I was fingerprinted and read my charges.

I was told I could post bail, which was $10,000. Luckily, I had quite a bit on me from the first hour of the swap, and since I wasn't really a flight risk, I only had to post 10%. I was detained all day. They didn't let me post bail until after the reptile swap had ended at 6:00 p.m.

Steve, nor my girlfriend, had any idea what was going on this whole time. I had the van, and they had no way to get home or transport the animals. They didn't know if I was coming back or not. They were left in the pole barn, where the swap is held every month...all alone. Everybody else had left much earlier. I had no way to get a hold of them, as we didn't have cell phones yet.

I finally arrived and explained what had happened to me. I let them know I had to drive back to appear in front of a judge regarding my charges. We packed all of our stuff back into the van and drove home. My court date was about two months later; I had talked to a few attorneys in the interim. I was the only one to get arrested...everybody else received fines.

When my court date arrived, I drove all the way back and appeared in front of the judge. I let him know I had spoken with numerous attorneys who told me this was a clear case of entrapment. The judge agreed it was definitely entrapment, which is illegal in Cook County. He felt sorry for the way I was treated, but let me know I didn't have a leg on which to stand. The maximum penalty was a prison sentence, so I wasn't as confident as when I had entered the courthouse. I assumed I would be released because entrapment was illegal.

The judge was really cool and admitted it looked like the agents just wanted money. He explained that what they did was perfectly legal, even though it was pretty crappy and underhanded. He only gave me a $100 fine and said I was free to go.

I never did take the time to get this expunged in court, so I think it's pretty funny that I probably have a criminal record for buying and selling endangered tortoises. Now you know the rest of the story.

Rambo

Rambo

My dad and Rambo

Diane bottle feeding Rambo

In the early 1980s, I was one of the largest breeders of greater bush babies in the United States. Greater bush babies are prosimians, which are lesser primates. They are native to Africa and are one of the most adorable animals in the world. They primarily live in the trees (arboreal), and they jump around when they are traveling on the ground. They have a long prehensile tail they use as a fifth limb, mainly for balance. They can't swing, or hang on with their tail like some other prehensile-tailed animals.

I always left the babies with their mom for at least ten days, so they got colostrums. I then bottle-fed them. I had a few wonderful breeder pairs, and we produced quite a few babies over the years. I named our very first baby, "Grasshopper," because of the way he jumped all over the house. He lived in our house and ate whatever my daughter and I had every night for dinner. He lived with us until he died from old age at 21-years-old.

I gave one of our babies to my sister and brother-in-law when they were married over 13 years ago, and they still have George now. George Bush (baby)…get it?

We named the bush baby in this story, "Rambo," because he had no fear at all. He would ride around on our Great Dane's back all the time. Rambo loved to be on our shoulders, and my wife was his favorite person. In fact, the Ann Arbor News came out and did a feature story on Animal Magic, and one of the pictures they put in their newspaper was of Rambo hiding in my wife's hair. Diane has a beautiful, full head of curly hair, and Rambo loved to burrow into it and just hang out. The photo showed Rambo's head looking like it was sticking out of the back of her head.

Rambo loved us and lived in the house with us. One of the bush babies' biggest drawbacks is they scent mark. Males would urinate on their hands, leaving their scent everywhere they touched.

114

The time came when that we couldn't keep this "scent-marking monkey" in our house anymore. We could only take so much of Rambo "marking" our furniture, our heads, our shoulders, etc., so I placed him in a large cage in our sanctuary. I was supplying pet shops with their reptiles, small mammals and birds at the time, and the owner of a pet shop in North Dakota drove all the way here to hand pick reptiles for his store. I won't use his actual name in this story for reasons that will be apparent as you keep reading. I'll call him, "Jim." Jim saw Rambo and fell in love. I told him Rambo wasn't for sale, but he kept pushing and pushing. I could see that Rambo really liked Jim, because he didn't want to go back in his cage. Rambo wouldn't leave Jim's shoulders.

I told Jim I would have to talk it over with my wife. Diane and I decided we would let Jim have Rambo, as long as we got him back if ever the time came when he couldn't care for him anymore. I told Jim I needed this in writing, and he agreed. I went over all the necessities with Jim. He told me Rambo would live with him at home and accompany him to his pet shop every day, sort of as their mascot. Jim promised he would never sell or trade Rambo, and he would treat Rambo like his son.

He left with his reptiles and his new store mascot, and that is the end of this story…or so I thought. Here's where it got weird. I received a phone call about three years later from a lady, who I'll call "Sue." She told me she was Jim's wife, and she wanted to know what to do with Rambo. I asked her if Rambo was sick; she stated he was doing great and lives in her house. I asked what the problem was. She told me Jim was having some health problems and had been hospitalized. She said Jim could no longer take care of Rambo, and Rambo didn't like her.

She asked if I would take Rambo back and I said, "Of course, we would be happy to have him back." She agreed to drive Rambo all the way to Michigan the following week, so I gave her directions.

I received another phone call a few days later from Jim, who asked me if his wife had called. I told him about our conversation and he said, "Please don't do that. Rambo is mine and I'm in the process of getting a divorce from Sue. I'm having some problems right now, and I'm in the hospital. My attorney is taking care of Rambo until I get out." I told him Rambo was his, and I would honor his wish to keep Rambo. His wife didn't have the authority to give Rambo back to me anyway…only Jim did. We had it in writing.

Again, that's the end of this story…or so we thought. I received another phone call from Sue a couple weeks after I had spoken with Jim. She told me she needed to have a serious talk to me. She said, "Jim is in a psychiatric hospital and is being physically restrained. He went crazy and tried to kill me. This is why we are getting divorced. Rambo doesn't like me anymore, and I can't take care of him."

Rambo had been running loose while under Jim's care, but Rambo was now locked inside a small bird cage. Sue went on to tell me Rambo was now acting crazy as well, and she was afraid of him. I told her I understood why Rambo would not be friendly anymore, since he was permanently locked up in a small cage. Sue asked if we could please take him back, and I told her Jim had called me a couple weeks earlier from the hospital. Sue was shocked; she had no idea how Jim could have called me from the hospital. She told me Jim had an attorney, and maybe his attorney had something to do with the call.

I told Sue that Jim had begged me not to let her get rid of Rambo. He told me Rambo was all he had left, and he loved Rambo more than anything. I told Sue I felt sorry for Jim. Sue then told me she could no longer care for Rambo and that her attorney said she now had power of attorney. She also said Jim wouldn't be getting out the hospital any time soon. I asked her to please have her attorney call me, and he did.

I told him I didn't know what to do, both legally and morally. I was thinking of Rambo's best interest, not Jim or Sue's best interest. Sue's attorney said Sue had the right to make any decision regarding Rambo, and he had the proper court documents to prove it. Sue didn't want any money for Rambo…she just wanted Rambo gone, because he kept trying to attack her.

I told Sue's attorney I would be more than happy to take Rambo back, as long as I had something signed stating I could legally take possession of Rambo. Sue's attorney said it would be no problem and had the papers prepared. Diane and Samantha, my wife and her daughter, decided to make the long journey to North Dakota to bring our "baby" back home. Diane and I were overjoyed that we would be seeing Rambo again; we couldn't wait!

Diane drove seventeen hours non-stop and called me when she arrived at Sue's house. Diane talked to Sue for awhile and got the proper documents. Rambo was already in a travel carrier when Diane arrived, so she put him in her car and started on the long trip back home. Diane decided to stop at a hotel in South Dakota for the night, because she had been driving for so long and was getting tired. Diane called me and asked if she could let Rambo out of his cage to run loose in the hotel room. I warned her not to do it. Diane thought Rambo would immediately jump on her shoulder and start kissing her like he used to, but I knew better.

I told her what to feed him, and I specifically told her not to open his cage door…to just put the food through the bars. I explained that Rambo no longer knew her, and he's been locked up in a small cage for a long time. Also, who knew what Jim did to Rambo? I knew Jim was in a psychiatric hospital, and maybe he wasn't telling the truth about how well he cared for Rambo.

Diane did as I asked, even though she really wanted to let Rambo out to play. She fed him through the bars and told me he looked really sad. She said to picture a person in jail hanging onto the bars and looking out. Rambo had his hands on the cage bars looking out with his sad eyes.

Diane arrived home the following day and brought Rambo's cage into our kitchen, because we both really wanted to see, hold and cuddle him. Because of my many years of experience working with animals, I learned never to trust them. I knew anything could happen at any given time. I told Diane I was going to open the cage and let Rambo out but to be prepared for anything. I had no idea what Rambo would do. Diane was going on about how much she missed him and how she couldn't wait to hold him. I could tell, just by looking at him, that Rambo wasn't the same mischievous baby as when he left us.

I opened the cage and Rambo shot out like a bullet. He came right at me. He rose up on his hind legs and started jumping around the kitchen, trying to attack me. I yelled for Diane to get upstairs and lock the door, while Rambo was chasing me around the kitchen. I'm sure this was a real sight to see! I'm positive Rambo was trying to kill me, not just chase me to play. He was hissing and growling. I don't remember how, but I eventually got him back into his cage without suffering too many bites.

Since bush babies are primates, their bites are really bad and infection is inevitable. I was treated and prescribed antibiotics. I called a couple of zoos I had dealt with and found Rambo a forever home as a breeder. One of the zoos I contacted had a couple of females and no male. They were overjoyed to get Rambo. I let them know how mean he was, and that he was no longer able to be handled. I didn't want them finding out the way I did.

I guess this story has a happy ending…we got Rambo out of a horrible situation where he was locked in a small cage and were able to place him in a permanent home where he could run around with his two new girlfriends!

Chivalry Is Dead

My sister, Debbie

I still owned The Reptile Source in 1991 and had animals in every room in my house. I mean there were cages everywhere. I personally delivered reptiles to some of my out-of-state pet stores about once a month. I mainly shipped them, but I would give pet shops a chance to hand pick their animals every now and then. I was heading out to Iowa, Missouri, Nebraska, Illinois and Indiana and was planning on being gone about a week.

My youngest sister, Debbie, volunteered to stay at my house and take care of my animals. Debbie would do anything for anyone; in fact, both of my sisters would. Debbie said she would stay there with her boyfriend to make sure everything was taken care of properly. She said she would feed my dog, my mammals and all the birds, but she wasn't even going in the reptile room. She isn't fond of snakes, and her boyfriend wasn't either.

Before I left, I told Debbie I wanted a phone call every night to let me know everything was ok. I always worried something would go wrong whenever I'm on the road. I never sleep until I get that reassuring call.

I received her phone call the first two nights, letting me know everything was ok. I was awakened by my phone ringing around 3:00 a.m. the second night. It was Debbie, who was completely hysterical! I told her to calm down and tell me what was wrong. She said that she and her boyfriend were awakened by a noise coming from the reptile room. They assumed a tortoise had escaped, so Debbie opened the door to see "Julius Squeezer," my eighteen-foot Burmese python, slithering towards them! Did I mention that Debbie had Ophidiophobia, a fear of snakes?

Debbie shut the door and immediately called me. She was freaking out! Neither she, nor her boyfriend, had any idea what to do. I told her that Jules, as I affectionately called this python, had to be placed back in his cage. Debbie had a different idea. She wanted to just shut the door and leave him loose in that room until I returned. I explained there was a good chance he would knock over other cages and potentially let venomous snakes out.

I told Debbie that Jules was friendly, and all she had to do was open the door, have her boyfriend pick Jules up and place him back in his cage...easier said than done! Debbie asked me if I had any gloves for her to wear and I asked her why. I asked what good gloves would do, because they were not going to stop an eighteen-foot snake. I'm not the most reassuring person. I told her to call me when Jules was back in his cage. Debbie's boyfriend, the big tough guy he was, opened the door and saw this massive python. He pushed Debbie into the room and shut the door!

Debbie was a real trooper and stepped up to the plate. She approached Jules, bent down to pick him up about a third of the way back from his head, and placed his head into the open door of his cage where he slithered right back into his home. She shut his cage door and latched it before calling me back. I guess I didn't check to make sure it was securely latched before I left.

Debbie called me after Jules was safely in his cage telling me how "chicken" her boyfriend was and what he had done. She said it took her about 25 minutes to get Jules back in his cage. I wanted to find a way to thank Debbie for helping me, so I thought I would put this story in my book.

Thanks again Debbie, that was very nice of you!

Left Me in Stitches

Here's another story that Steve just reminded me of that occurred in the early 1990s. I had moved The Reptile Source out of my house and into a 20,000 square-foot building in Romulus, Michigan. At the time, I had the largest lizard in the United States...an over nine-foot long Salvator water monitor named Mongo. I had him flown in from the Toronga Zoo in Australia. These lizards are known to mellow out as they age, but Mongo was an exception. He would defecate, take his massive tail and fling his crap right at us! His aim was extremely accurate, and I can't count how many times we were showered with excrement.

Most monitors are known for having numerous strains of dangerous bacteria in their saliva. Getting bitten usually requires a trip to the doctor's office for antibiotics. I was teaching Steve how to feed large lizards on this particular day. I always feed frozen rodents that are thawed out first. There is no reason to feed live food, because you risk your animal's safety by doing so. I can't count how many phone calls I've received over the years from people who put live mice and rats in their reptile's cage, only to come back later and find a live rodent feeding on their dead reptile.

I don't remember why I was feeding Mongo a mouse, because I should have been feeding him a guinea pig or chicken at his size. A mouse for Mongo was like a marshmallow for me. I think I had a few extra mice thawed out that day, which was probably why I used them. In hindsight, I should have just put them back in the freezer.

I held the mouse up by its tail while turning toward Steve. I never want anybody to get injured, so I sternly told Steve, "Don't ever do anything I do…especially don't do this." As I said the word, "this," Mongo leapt up and tried to grab the mouse. He didn't get the mouse, but he did get my index finger, almost severing it from the rest of my hand. Blood started spurting everywhere! I had to wrap my hand in a towel before driving to the hospital. No worries…almost everyone at our local hospital knew me on a first-name basis! I received eleven stitches and learned my lesson…I now practice what I preach!

The Doe and Joe

I received a phone call from a Van Buren police officer at about nine o'clock at night on August 17, 2012. Most of you will never experience anything like this. The officer told me they had a distraught citizen who would only speak to me. The officer asked if I had ever heard of "Joe Smith." I changed his name in this story for obvious reasons.

I answered, "No, should I?"

She replied, "He's the town drunk." I asked if he rides around on a bicycle picking up bottles and cans. She replied positively, so I said I knew who he was.

Joe had called me years ago from a bait shop. He asked to use their phone to call me, because he saw a pink kangaroo in the woods where he was camping. He's a Vietnam War veteran who had no family or home, so he usually slept in the woods behind the car wash in Belleville. He's a loner who has Post Traumatic Stress Disorder, as well as, a bunch of other problems.

I met him by the railroad tracks in Belleville and asked him where this kangaroo was. Joe was always drunk, but he attempted to show me where he spotted the kangaroo in the woods. I followed him and searched for over an hour, but obviously didn't find a pink kangaroo.

Back to this story...I used to save all my returnable pop cans to give to Joe whenever I saw him. I wanted him to get the money, which is probably why he requested me. The police officer asked if I would call Joe and try to calm him down. I asked why, and she said a deer had been hit by a vehicle in front of Joe's cabin. Years earlier, the city collected donations to help Joe out, since he served our country for years, and he had no family to help. They got him a little cabin on Haggerty Road in Belleville. It's a sufficient house, with running water, heat and a phone.

Joe called the police to get a kill permit, so he could keep it for food. The police arrived and issued Joe the kill permit. Joe called back about an hour later to say there was a fawn in the deer, and it was moving. He said it started moving just as he started to slice open the deer's belly.

Joe said, "I want to talk to the guy with red hair who has animals all over his van. I want to talk to him before I do anything." The police knew who I was and gave me a call. The officer asked if I would call Joe and set his mind at ease. I asked the officer if the deer was dead, explaining that a baby can't live if it's mother is dead. She told me to hang on while she called the officer at the scene.

She got back to me after talking with the officer. I said the deer was definitely dead. They received the original call at 6:30 a.m. It was now past 9:30 a.m., which means the deer had been dead for hours. I agreed to call him.

I called and immediately realized he was inebriated. Keep in mind this was only about 10:15 in the morning. I said, "Hi, this is Mark with Animal Magic. Is this Joe?"

He responded, slurring his words, "Yesh, I got a problem here."

I asked, "Joe, are you sure the deer is dead?"

In response he said, "I was feeding it this morning. As I was watching, a car came around the corner and hit it. I dragged it back over to my house and called the police. The deer wasn't dead yet." I wondered how he dragged an adult deer that was still alive back to his house with his bare hands.

Joe then said, "When I went to slice open its belly, it started kicking, right where its business is." I knew where he meant.

I said, "It's probably bloat, because gasses build up…"

He interrupted me saying, "No, I'm telling ya', there's a baby, and I don't know what to do."

I said, "Well, I would cut open the mom…"

He cut me off again saying, "No, I ain't gonna have nothing to do with no abortion."

I responded, "Joe, it's not abortion. Abortion is when you terminate the life of a fetus. This is actually trying to save the baby's life, so you're fine."

Joe said, "Well, can you come out and do it, because I wouldn't feel right about doing it."

I objected, "Joe, I'm heading out to perform for the Salvation Army in Flint, and I can't come out there right now. I'll make you a deal. Cut open the deer; see if there's a baby. If there is, and if it's alive, then call me. Here is my phone number. I will either send someone over, or I will come by later."

He said, "But her business is moving and I don't know what to do. I wouldn't feel right…"

I cut him off and calmly said, "Don't worry about it Joe. You are going to save the baby."

He said, "Well, I'll do whatever I got to do."

I responded, "Let me know how it turns out. I'm sure everything will be fine." He was very appreciative and thanked me. It was very hard to understand him, because of the state he was in.

Joe never called back, and I haven't heard from him since. I'm assuming there was no baby, or I would have heard back from him.

The Other Man

Back in June of 2012, I was attempting to convert some VHS movies into DVDs, but I couldn't figure out how to do it. They were a bunch of animal rescues I had done from over the years that I wanted to condense onto one DVD. After many tries, and quite a few words I can't print here, I could only get them to play on my computer, not in a DVD player. I called Tim, a friend of mine who repairs computers asking him what I could do. Since I'm on his caller ID, he knew it was me and answered, "Hey Mark."

I said, "Hey Tim, I need some help, and I figure you're the man to call. I can't get my computer to make DVDs. I tried to burn them with the program you gave me, and I've been working on this for hours. I'm really getting frustrated and have no idea what to do. Every time I try it, I get these prompts and don't understand them. I follow them; it still doesn't work. It takes forever to complete. I then find out they don't play in my DVD player, only on my computer. What do I do?"

Tim responded, "Mark, I have no clue what you are talking about. What do you want me to do?"

I said, "Tim, I figured you were the guy to call to tell me what to do."

He stated, "No, I don't know what to do."

I said, "OK, thanks anyway; I'll keep trying to figure it out. I'll talk to you later."

I decided to call him back about half-an-hour later. I looked at my phone to press redial. It was at this moment that I realized, and this is extremely embarrassing, that I have two different friends named Tim. One is a police officer with the Northville Township Police Department; the other is a computer repairman.

They are both listed alphabetically under "Tim" in my phone. My eyes aren't as good as they used to be, so when I scrolled down the names in my phone looking for "Tim, the computer guy," I accidentally called, "Tim, the police officer."

Well, he has me on Caller ID in his phone, so of course he answers, "Hi Mark."

I said, "Hey Tim." He knows it's me, and I assume its Tim, the computer guy. I asked this police officer all these questions for at least ten minutes. He was as nice as he could be. Now it makes sense why he told me he didn't know what I was talking about.

I kept telling him, throughout the phone call, that he was "the man" and that he must know what to do. It dawned on me that I had the wrong Tim, when I hit redial. I called Tim, the police officer, to apologize and explain what I had done, but I got his voice mail. Now I'm thinking that he doesn't want to talk to me anymore, because he thinks I'm some lunatic!

I left him a long message explaining what had happened. I haven't heard from him since. I hope everything is fine and there are no hard feelings. I know he read my first book, so I really hope he reads this one also. Tim, if you are reading this, I promise to only call you regarding police matters in the future!

Furby

I received a phone call in 2008 from Romulus Animal Control regarding a fledgling owl someone had found. It had a few feathers and probably fell out of a tree. I told them I would take it and try my best to raise it up, rehab it, and hopefully, set it free where it belongs.

This was the youngest owl I had ever attempted to raise. I immediately identified it as a great horned owl. It wasn't real friendly, nor did I expect it to be. There is no way this baby would have survived on its own in the wild. It could barely open its eyes. We named him "Furby," because he looked exactly like one of those popular kids' toys.

I had to feed him pinky (baby) mice, and Furby was so small that I had to "break" the mice into little pieces. I don't feed live mice, so I thaw out frozen ones. I had to cut these mice up into little pieces. Yes, it was as gross as you're imagining right now! I learned it's easier, and less messy, to cut them with wire cutters while they are still frozen. It sounds gross, but you do what needs to be done to save an animal's life. I would feed this little guy tiny pieces of baby mice, with tweezers, many times throughout the day.

Birds need to eat quite often, because their metabolism is so high. I kept doing this until Furby grew so big that he progressed to full-sized pinkie mice, then fuzzy mice, then weanling mice, until he eventually was large enough to eat adult mice.

I decided Furby was finally able to be released about five-months later, when he was eating adult mice on his own. We hadn't handled him at all, because we wanted him to be able to live on his own in the wild. I wanted him to have a natural fear of humans. The day came when it was time for Furby to be released. We drove him to a local nature preserve, and I opened his crate, while my wife and I said our good-byes. We were extremely attached to him, since he was raised in our house. As Furby took a couple of steps out of the crate, he flapped his massive wings, and was gone, never to be seen again...or so we thought.

The following summer, almost a full year later, a neighbor who lives about half-a-mile down the road, knocked on my door. I had no idea who it was, so I asked, "May I help you?"

The man answered, "I know you're the animal guy, and we have a large owl that seems injured in our cornfield. We knew you would know what to do."

I replied that I didn't want to go on a wild goose chase trying to catch an owl in the middle of a cornfield, but the man said, "We already caught it. We put a large garbage can over it, and it's still in the field." I told him I would try my best to help.

I followed him to his place, after loading up my thick, owl-handling gloves and a carrier, as well as, a net...just in case. I went into his cornfield and carefully tilted up the garbage can. I observed an adult great horned owl, which is one of the most magnificent animals in the world and extremely impressive to see. I opened the animal carrier and set it on the ground. Here's the amazing thing: this owl took a couple steps toward me and walked right into the carrier! I kid you not! I remember it like it happened yesterday. I then realized this owl was Furby. No wild owl would ever walk into an animal carrier like that.

I know it sounds hard to believe, but I know this owl was Furby. He had no fear of me and actually seemed happy in the carrier. He didn't hiss, attempt to bite or even flap his wings. The man and his family were all watching and couldn't believe what they were witnessing. I told him about Furby, and explained that we raised him from a baby and he obviously remembered me.

I drove him to our sanctuary and took him to Dr. Scott. We X-rayed him, and she told me he had a few fractured bones in one of his wings. He probably hit a phone line, tree or a car. I can't believe this owl had fallen right back in my lap for the second time in a year. Dr. Scott bandaged his wing and gave me antibiotics that had to be administered three times a day for 14 days.

Furby was now eating small rats, and it got to the point where he was ready to be released for the second time. Furby was now much older than the first time we released him, much wiser, larger, and it seemed like he knew I was trying to help him. The day came when he was to be released, so we did the same thing as the previous year. I opened the carrier and he walked out, turned around, as if to say good-bye and flapped his wings. We never saw him again.

What a great feeling it is to release an animal back where it belongs!

Roach Motel

I traveled to Missouri on September 22, 2010 to attend a zoo auction. I was hoping there would be a few animals I might be able to use in my educational performances. I was too tired to drive all the way back, so I stopped at a motel in Normal, Illinois around midnight.

I won't say the name of the motel chain, but I got stuck in the motel room from Hell! I've stayed in hundreds of hotels and motels over the years, but this was, by far, the worst one ever. I asked the clerk for a non-smoking room for two reasons: I can't stand the smell, and more importantly, I'm extremely allergic. She said, "No problem," and gave me a non-smoking room.

I drove to the room and noticed a "NO SMOKING" sign on the door. I unlocked the door and proceeded to open it. The heavy smell of cigarettes hit me. The room reeked, and I noticed an ashtray on the little side table full of cigarette butts. I called the front desk to complain. She apologized, stating it was their only room available. I had no choice, because I was so tired. I brought in my luggage and animals. I had a baby bear with me, who needed his bottle every few hours, as well as, numerous reptiles and a couple of large birds.

I went to wash my hands and make the bear's formula, only to discover the water didn't work: neither the cold nor the hot. I decided to just use the bathtub's faucet, which I did, only to discover that the bathtub wouldn't drain. I looked around for a plunger; of course, there was none. I then saw that the bathtub was draining, just extremely slowly. I used the bathtub's tap to get water for the animals and to brush my teeth.

The carpet in this room was so heavily stained that I really had no clue what its original color was. I don't think it had been cleaned in years. I didn't want to walk on it barefoot, so I kept my socks on until I sat on the bed.

Another big problem was the phone next to the bed. It had a red light on top that wouldn't stop flashing. There must have been a message, which caused it to continually flash…all night long! I called the front desk and asked how to turn off the flashing light. The clerk apologized and told me the person who had the room before me must have had a voice message that he, or she, didn't receive. The clerk had no idea how to retrieve it, or how to turn off the light. I tried covering it with a towel, but the light was shining right through it.

Here's another problem: I'm an animal lover who owns all kinds of animals…but I don't like them crawling on me in the middle of the night! This room was infested with cockroaches, which I didn't notice, because they only come out in the dark. They came out every time I turned off the light, making it impossible for me to sleep. I even had them falling on me from the ceiling, while I was lying down on the bed!! I couldn't sleep at all. I even turned the television on, hoping the light from it would keep the cockroaches hidden. That didn't work either.

Every time I would dose off and then awaken, I would see numerous cockroaches on the walls, the ceiling and the bed. I hope you are getting the willies while reading this, so you will at least get a taste of what I experienced that night. I got out of bed at 5:00 a.m., because it was fruitless for me to try and sleep. I took a shower and had to make it quick, because the water in the bathtub was going to overflow.

I went to check out at the front desk and explained everything that had gone wrong to the clerk. She told me the manager had already comped my room, and my credit card wouldn't get charged. I said thanks, but that wasn't the point. Nobody should have to go through what I did.

Think about this story the next time any of you are in Normal, Illinois.

Road Warriors

I received a phone call in July of 2004, to perform at a large corporate event at The Grand Traverse Resort in Traverse City. It was a very ritzy place, and I was offered a lot of money to perform. The only problem was the date coincided with one of my two weeks away with my family. We rent the same cabin every year, and this was during one of the weeks we were to be up there.

We leave on a Saturday and stay until the following Saturday morning. This company wanted me the Saturday night we were to leave for Houghton Lake. Traverse City is over five hours away from our sanctuary, but only about two hours away from Houghton Lake. I figured I would take the job and bring some of my easier animals to care for, which I would keep with us in our cabin for the week.

I brought a baby kangaroo that I was bottle feeding. I planned to house her in a portable baby playpen. I also brought Seven, the largest sloth in the United States. Sloths are easy to care for, and she travels everywhere with me. They sleep twenty-hours a day and only go potty once-a-week. Seven usually hangs upside down on the curtain rod above the shower. I also brought a fairly large alligator that I planned to keep in the bathtub, when we weren't using it, of course. I would place it in a large crate while we were in the shower. The other animals consisted of a large tarantula and a tri-color milk snake, both of which would be extremely easy to care for in our cabin.

Our dogs always travel with us, and this trip was no exception. We had two Great Danes, a 205 pounder named Tinker and a larger one named Akbar. We also traveled with Abby, my wife's black Labrador who was pretty old at the time. We didn't have any real young children at the time, only our eight-year-old and our 13-year-old daughters, and they stayed in the cabin right next to ours with the dogs.

All of the animals rode in the van with us. Our luggage and beach toys went in a small trailer that I towed.

As we were about to drive by East Lansing in my old purple...yes, you read that right...purple mini-van, my "check engine" light came on. Soon after, smoke started pouring out from under the van, and the engine died. I coasted onto the shoulder, right under the Trowbridge Exit bridge, and I tried to restart the van. Nothing happened. I had no idea what to do. Remember, not only did I have three other people with me, but I also had all the animals. It was extremely hot outside!

I used my cell phone to call John, a friend of mine who owns a repair shop, and told him what had happened. He told me he would look at it, but I needed to get it towed to him. He was about 75 miles away from where we were stranded. I called AAA, because I am a member, entitling me to 100 miles of free towing.

I called AAA and was told they could come out and tow my van, but not the trailer. I had to disconnect our trailer, with all of our stuff in it, and leave it under the bridge. I realized that once AAA arrived and towed my van, we would be stranded with the trailer and all of our exotic animals, as well as, our three massive dogs.

I had no idea what to do; this was way before internet access and smart phones. I had a cell phone, but could only make and receive phone calls. I remembered a U-Haul rental facility in East Lansing, only a few miles ahead of us, from my days at Michigan State. I thought we could all fit in a U-Haul to drive the remaining two hours. I called information and requested their phone number. I called, knowing most businesses would be closed for the weekend. I got lucky, and someone answered their phone.

The company told me they only had one larger U-Haul left, but I had to drive to them to get it. This U-Haul was way bigger than what we needed, but it was all they had available. The man who answered the phone didn't speak English very well, but I told him that I definitely wanted the U-Haul. I asked if he could bring it out to where we were, and he said he could pick me up and bring me to their location. I thought this was weird, but again, I didn't have much of a choice.

Two very large men arrived in a U-Haul about thirty minutes later, neither one of them speaking English very well. Both seemed pretty upset. I assumed they would bring two vehicles. I would fill out their paperwork and pay, and they could take the second vehicle back, leaving the other one for us. That's not what happened.

They climbed out of their U-Haul and said, "Come with us." I asked why, and they told me we had to go back to the office. They needed to run my credit card, perform a background check, copy my driver's license, and fill out the paperwork.

I didn't feel comfortable leaving my girlfriend, our kids, our dogs, our luggage, our trailer and the exotic animals on the side of the freeway. Diane told me to go with them, and everything would be fine. She is always so rational.

The larger of the two men got in the driver's side, and the other guy told me to get in the truck. I did as I was told and was now wedged between these two behemoths in the front seat of the U-Haul. To make matters worse, this U-Haul was a stick shift.

It was right out of a horror movie! I looked back and waved goodbye...assuming it was for the very last time...as we drove off into the sunset. I had no idea where they were really taking me and not a word was spoken in English the entire ride. I thought, "Great, they're going to kill me and send someone back for the girls." Since I was trained in Martial Arts, I anticipated how I would defend myself, should something happen. I was thinking about which one I would subdue first, and how I was going to do it. I decided not to take out the driver first, because we would crash. I would go after the other one. All these thoughts went through my head.

We pulled into an alley near Frandor Mall, which is in a really bad area of East Lansing. We stopped and the driver said, "Get out," as the other guy opened his door and exited.

I got out and thought to myself, "This is it...I'm about to be shot."

The bigger guy walked to a door and unlocked it. He told me to come in and I saw we were now in the back of a U-Haul rental center.

I filled out all of their paperwork and paid, without noticing how much time had gone by. I had no way to contact Diane, because I left my cell phone with her, just in case something happened, and she needed it. I drove the U-Haul back down I-96 heading North, knowing I would have to exit and come back Southbound to get them. This whole time I was thinking, "Is my family still there? Are they all right? Are the animals fine?"

As I approached, I noticed my purple van was still under the bridge. The tow truck arrived right when I pulled up to the van. We took the animals out of the van and put them in the back of the U-Haul. We then took everything else out of the trailer and put it in the U-Haul, as well.

It was at this point that I found out that Jessica, my twelve-year-old daughter, had to go to the bathroom while I was gone. On the way, we had stopped at a 7-Eleven. She drank a large Slurpee and couldn't hold it in any longer. Remember, the three of them were stranded under this bridge, with nowhere to walk within eyesight. Jessie decided to walk a little way from the highway, into the woods, to relieve herself. She did her business and walked back. Diane then told her that a bunch of construction workers were on top of the bridge, and they could all see what Jessie had done!

Back to the story. I remember this very vividly, because I was extremely worried about all the animals. U-Hauls don't have air-conditioning in the back, nor do they have any ventilation. We had no choice but to try and make the best of the situation.

One other problem…we had four people and only one seat. It's illegal to drive with more than three people in the front seat of any vehicle, but again, we had no choice. I left the empty trailer under the bridge, thinking someone would steal it, and I lifted all three dogs into the back of this massive U-Haul. Abby was easy to lift, because she was only about 65 pounds. The Danes were another story. I finally got them in; then the four of us piled into the front seat. I drove with Jessie who sat next to me, and Sam sat on Diane's lap.

I started to drive and wondered what I would do about my performance in Traverse City that evening. There was no way I could drive this giant U-Haul all the way there…the gas alone would cost a fortune. I remembered there was a car rental by the Lansing Airport, so we decided to drive there and look into renting an additional vehicle.

We arrived at the airport where I explained our situation to the clerk, purposely leaving out the part about all the animals. We rented a nice-sized SUV for the week. The rental agent was extremely kind giving us a great rate with unlimited mileage, as long as we didn't leave the state. This SUV even had a trailer hitch!

It was too late to go back for the trailer, because I had to be in Traverse City to perform that evening. I drove the U-Haul with Jessie, while Diane followed in the SUV with Sam. We were now about two hours behind schedule.

We pulled over at every rest area, and anywhere else we could find, to open up the bay door of the U-Haul. It was extremely hot outside! I wanted to give the animals some fresh air and the dogs' water as often as possible. I was extremely worried, especially about the dogs. Great Danes overheat very quickly, and Abby was quite old. I didn't want anything to happen to them.

It was an extremely stressful drive, but we eventually made it to Houghton Lake. We unloaded everything into our cabins and gave all the animals water. After giving the little roo his bottle, I drove the U-Haul another hour-and-a-half to Roscommon, where we dropped it off. Diane followed in the SUV. I paid a little more for a one-way rental, but we still had the SUV to drive for the week and didn't need to spend any more money on the U-Haul.

We were done with the U-Haul (what a relief!), but I still had a couple of problems: I had no idea if my trailer was still under the overpass, and we had no way to get back home at the end of the week.

The SUV wasn't large enough for all of us, the dogs, our supplies and all the animals.

We decided to leave the girls at Houghton Lake, since my parents had a cabin within walking distance, and they were already there. Diane and I would drive back to get the trailer, if it was still there, and then return to the cabin. Keep in mind, I still had to drive and perform in Traverse City later on that evening.

Diane drove with me to keep me company. We were both straining our eyes as we approached the Trowbridge Exit. Would the trailer still be there? We had no idea, until Diane spotted it. We got off the exit and turned around to arrive at the trailer. I checked to see if it would fit on the SUV's hitch. We had a 50/50 chance, since there are two sizes of trailer hitches, and it fit! I hooked it up and off we went, back to Houghton Lake.

We arrived there...again, where I unhitched the trailer and left it outside our cabin. I fed the baby kangaroo and loaded the animals into the SUV. I was now on a very tight time constraint, as I had to leave right away for Traverse City. Diane, once again, decided to keep me company, and off we went.

I was scheduled to start my show at tcn p.m., and we arrived a little after nine, leaving me just enough time to set up. Everything went great and everyone had a wonderful time. They were so impressed that they booked me for the following year before I left.

We arrived back at our cabin around 2:00 a.m., very relieved that the day was finally over. The rest of our week went fine, except for Diane. She has an intense fear of alligators and had to deal with a four-footer in our bathtub all week. I put him in a crate every time she needed to use the bathroom.

I drove the rental SUV to my friend's auto shop when we arrived back home. John was behind the counter when I walked in, and I asked him how much I owed him. He said I owed him nothing. I asked what was wrong with the van, when he said I didn't take it out of overdrive. I didn't remember to do that, and you need to when towing anything. I caused it to overheat by leaving it in overdrive, which did no damage at all. John just added some transmission fluid, and it was fine. Nothing was damaged at all, except for my pride. All I had to do was push the little button on the end of the gear shift before driving the first morning. This entire story would have been avoided!

Since we got such a great deal on the SUV, Diane used it for traveling the following week to Philadelphia. We kept it for another two weeks after she arrived back home. We finally returned it to the

Detroit Metropolitan Airport's car return one month after first renting it. What a deal!

ICP

Shaggy 2 Dope   Shaggy, DJ Clay, Me & Widget

I received a phone call from the President of Psychopathic Records in November, 2011. He wanted to know if I owned a monkey they could use for The Insane Clown Posse's newest video. This band, also known as ICP, hails from Detroit and has followers called "Juggalos" all over the U.S. They are very well known and the F.B.I. has actually deemed them, and their fans, a gang. The ICP is known for wearing black and white face paint, raunchy lyrics, and spraying bottles of Faygo Red Pop on the crowds at their concerts.

I'm not a fan of theirs, nor am I familiar with any of their songs. The ICP consists of Violent J and Shaggy 2 Dope. DJ Clay is their disc jockey. I was told they were launching a new web site, and they wanted me to bring a monkey to perform various things for the introduction. I told them it wasn't a problem. I would do it, as long as everything was safe for the monkey. I would be the only one working with her for the entire shoot.

We set up a date for me to drive down to their studio with Widget, my black and white ruffed lemur. Once I told my daughter where I was going, she asked if she could tag along with Carlos, her boyfriend, who loved The Insane Clown Posse. I justified bringing him, because he taught martial arts. I could say he was my body guard and that Jessica was one of my animal handlers.

We arrived about half-an-hour early, so I decided to wait in the parking lot until ten o'clock. A gold Cadillac with a moon roof pulled up, and a man who was covered in tattoos got out. The Insane Clown Posse is like Kiss. People don't know what they look like without their make-up. I noticed this man was wearing a necklace with a silver hatchet pendant, as he approached my van. Carlos told me this was their logo…the hatchet man. My van is covered with animal decals and is impossible not to notice. He knocked on my window, which I opened. He introduced himself as Joey, so I shook his hand and told him who we were. I had no idea who Joey was at the time; he said to come inside for the shoot. I closed my window and Carlos informed me that Joey was really Shaggy 2 Dope. I was surprised at how nice Joey was, given the ICP's reputation.

We went in and were introduced to a couple of cameramen and DJ Clay. I asked what they wanted me to do. They said they really wanted a shot of Widget holding a microphone, as if she was talking into it. They said they would edit it to look like all their fans, who had black and white face paint, were looking up to Widget, as she was looking down on them. It sounded cool because Widget was also black and white.

I told them, "No problem. Is the microphone expensive?" They asked me why I asked. I said my idea was to rub some marshmallow on the tip of the microphone, so Widget would hold it by the handle and lick the tip, making it look like she was talking into it. They told me the microphone wasn't a prop, that it was very expensive, but to go ahead and try. I had brought a bag of marshmallows with me, just in case, so I put the marshmallow on the tip of the mike. It worked to perfection. Widget raised the microphone to her mouth, and it looked like she was talking right into it.

I thought we were done, until they told me the next shot would be to get her to control the knobs on their sound board. They brought out this large contraption, which made me start to think. I asked them how it would look if I crouched down behind the sound board, which was on a counter, to use my hands to hold Widget's elbows to move her hands. I wanted to make sure I was out of the shot. I learned to get creative from filming so many commercials. We decided to try it, and it couldn't have worked any better. You can't see me at all in the finished product. They zoomed in on Widget's hands. It looked like she was moving all the dials and levers by herself.

We were only there for about an hour; everything went smoothly. All the guys were extremely down-to-Earth and very friendly. Shaggy 2 Dope asked if he could have a photo with Widget and me, so, of course I said yes. DJ Clay wanted one too, as did all the cameramen. The photo accompanying this story is Joey, who is Shaggy 2 Dope, without his make-up.

White Out

I was headlining the Columbus Pet Expo in 2008, and it just so happened that we had to drive through the worse blizzard in Ohio's history. It was so bad that the police actually closed the whole city of Columbus. You weren't allowed to be on the streets at all. We got to our hotel room, barely, and had no idea how bad it was going to get that night. We awakened to about four-feet of snow and had no clue that the police had declared Columbus an emergency zone.

I somehow managed to get our animals loaded into the van and attempted the drive to the Expo Center, which was about five miles away from our hotel. I have never seen anything like this before…cars were stuck everywhere…in the middle of major roads, in parking lots, everywhere. I don't know how, but I managed to get out of the hotel's parking lot, where we made it to the main street. I stopped at the only open gas station and bought a couple dozen donuts for the other vendors and performers, along with some coffee and drinks for us. We miraculously made it to the Expo Center, where we were informed that the city was being forced to close down. Most of the vendors had slept on the floor at the center because they knew better than to try to drive in the blizzard.

We gave the donuts to the vendors and started to set up our area. A few of them came over and told us everyone was bored and upset because the public wasn't allowed out of their houses. I decided to perform my Animal Magic show just for the vendors, because we were all stuck there for the weekend. I thought it would be nice and give everyone something to do. Not only aren't these vendors getting paid, but they were actually losing money at this expo.

Vendors don't get paid at these types of events; it's just the opposite. They have to pay thousands of dollars for their booths, which they recoup by selling whatever it is they have. Remember, there were no people at this expo at all, only the other vendors and performers. The performers are supposed to get paid when the expo is over, whether people are there or not. I wanted to make sure I got paid before we left, because we were warned that the lady in charge was known for not paying her performers in a timely manner.

After my first performance, one of the vendors, who looked like a witch, came up to my wife and said, "Snakes are evil, and I know this to be true because I killed one and it wouldn't die. It kept coming back to life every night." She said she witnessed it firsthand, and our snakes reminded her of her youth, when this supposedly happened. I got her to come over, and after much coaxing, she actually pet one of our larger pythons.

I performed numerous shows over the weekend, all for the same people. We started packing up our supplies and animals, once the expo was over on Sunday night, when we heard some of the other performers complaining about the lady in charge not paying them. They were told that she didn't make enough money, and she would send everyone checks the following week. This was her first ever major pet expo and she lost over $100,000. She paid for television and radio ads, billboards and newspaper ads, as well as, renting out the fairgrounds. There were no people paying, so she had no way to recoup what she had spent.

I went to her office four times, and she wouldn't open the door. I was told she wasn't there on the fifth attempt, but I'm pretty persistent. I finally got her on the sixth try. She told me she would send me a check the following week, and I told her that wasn't our deal. A number of vendors had told me earlier that this lady loved my shows and wanted me back every year. I used this knowledge to my advantage and told her I was never doing another one of her expos if I didn't get paid before I left. I couldn't believe it when she actually told me to hang on while she got my money. She came back and paid me, which I really didn't think was going to happen. I later found out that I was the only one who received any money at all.

She had me back the following year and I brought seven employees with me, as well as, some of our more unique animals. The crowds were magnificent! I even wrote a couple of chapters in my first book, "Animal Magic," about that experience. You can read about what happened in our hotel room with my wife and Beefy-T Bad Boy in that book.

As we were driving back to Michigan through this horribly blizzard, relieved to finally be done with this expo, I noticed flashing blue and red lights in my rear-view mirror. I was pulled over by an Ohio State Trooper, because unbeknownst to me, one of the tail lights on my trailer was burned out.

This officer was extremely nice and asked about all the animal decals covering the van. She asked what I did and what animals I had with me. I explained and told her from where we had just come. She ended up not giving me a citation and told me to drive carefully. She even gave us a shortcut to get home.

We eventually arrived back about eight hours later and our "trip from Hell" was finally over.

Wrong Turn

Who else, but me, could leave at 10:30 a.m. to perform at a six-year-old's birthday party in Michigan and end up in another country by 12:30 p.m.?

I packed up my animals and headed out to perform at a birthday party in Fort Gratiot, Michigan in 2012. I love what I do, but I really hate driving. This was a four-hour trip...two hours each way. I was following the instructions from my GPS and had already driven about two hours. I was less than four miles away from my destination, when my GPS told me to veer right. I turned and looked up to see I was now in a long line to drive over the Blue Water Bridge into Canada.

There was no way to turn around or get out of line, and I wasn't happy! I had no choice but to pay the toll to drive across the bridge into Canada, pulling over to the side just before reaching the custom's checkpoint. I got out of my van and stopped traffic, not knowing what else to do. I knew I couldn't bring these animals across the border, yet I couldn't just turn around.

A guard came running out of the custom's booth and yelled at me, "Get back in your vehicle! What do you think you are doing?" He was extremely belligerent.

I stated, "I arrived here by accident and…"

He cut me off by saying, "Get back in your car NOW!"

I did as he said and drove up to the Canadian custom's booth. I explained what had happened and told him I didn't want to enter Canada. I said I had exotic animals with me, and I'm licensed to have them. I proceeded to explain that I was late for a little girl's birthday party in Fort Gratiot, MI. He ordered, "Pull over there to the left and wait until someone comes for you."

While I was waiting (25 minutes later), I called the lady who had hired me to explain why I wasn't there yet. She told me she had two men who worked for homeland security at her party and wanted to know if I needed any help. I said I didn't know what was going to happen, but I had to go because two men were approaching my van.

One of the men said, "Turn around and go back over the bridge where they will be waiting for you." These guys moved a barrier and had me turn around without passing through customs. I guess you have to look at the bright side... at least I didn't have to pay twice. I got back to the United States side, where a guard was waiting for me. I drove over to where he was pointing. He approached my van and handed me a laminated card. He told me to wait until someone got me for security detail.

I had no clue what was going on or how much trouble I was in. A guard came out, about twenty minutes later, and asked if I had exotic animals in my van. I told him I did and that I was late for a birthday party. He asked what kinds of animals I had with me. I told him that I had all different kinds. At this point, he got on his walkie-talkie and told someone, "Hey, listen, I got a van here with all kinds of exotic animals. What should I do?" He came back over to me and said I had to wait until security could search my van.

I waited another twenty minutes until a lady came over and introduced herself as Vicky. She was really cool and had already researched me online. She saw the animal decals on my van, as well as, my web site. She decided to check my credentials. She said, "Listen, I checked you out and you're going to be fine. We have to send you to lane four. There is a lady waiting to search your van. She doesn't really want to, because she's scared of snakes, but she said she will." Vicky then asked me, "When was the last time you updated your GPS?"

I replied, "You have to update your GPS? I've never done that." She told me they had recently created a detour, and if you didn't update your GPS, you would be routed over the bridge into Canada. Once your GPS was updated, you would be taken on the detour to bypass the bridge.

I drove over to lane four and saw the line backed up over the bridge all the way to the Canadian side. Vicky arrived and stopped the cars so I could cut in, which was really nice of her. I drove up to the booth where a man was waiting, not a lady. He told me she had left because she was too scared. This agent was really nice and said, "Listen, I don't want to know what you have back there. I don't want to look at them. I'm going to let you through."

He let me pass, and I called the lady who had hired me to let her know I was still on the way. She told me not to worry because her homeland security friends had already called customs. They knew I was in lane four and had me pushed through it. I told her I wished I had known, because the stress had been killing me.

I arrived to the party over an hour late and was introduced to the two men who expedited my trip. Luckily, everyone was relaxed and not upset about my late arrival; the party went great!

Welcome to Our Nightmare

Back in December of 2008, I was hired to perform at a Christmas party for a huge corporation in Wisconsin. It was a long drive, way past Milwaukee, and I hadn't ever gone that far before to perform. I travel all over the United States now, but back then, I mainly performed in Michigan and Ohio.

This company offered me more than I had ever been paid for a one-hour performance, so I couldn't say no. They wanted me to start at 10:00 p.m., so I figured I would leave in the afternoon, drive all day, perform, and then head back to Michigan. I checked online and found that it would take me a little over nine hours to get there. I would also gain an hour on the way, because of the time zone difference.

My wife, being the nice woman she is, told me she would go with me to help out with the driving. James, our son, was only one-year-old at the time and was with us in his car seat. He was in the back seat with the animals all secure in their carriers behind him. My van has auxiliary heat and air in the rear to make sure the animals were comfortable.

The weather in Michigan was awful when we left, and the snow was really coming down. We knew this was going to be a bad trip right about the time we crossed the Indiana border. We had gone about 200 miles when Jamie started whining and complaining, which he never does. James is the best son anyone could ever ask for, so we knew something was wrong. Tinker, our 205-pound Great Dane, was lying beside Jamie on the back seat, when all of a sudden, Jamie threw up all over his clothes AND Tinker. There wasn't much we could do, because it was too late to turn back. To make matters worse, we didn't have a change of clothes for James, because we didn't anticipate this to happen.

I pulled onto the shoulder where Diane took off Jamie's clothes cleaning him with some wet wipes I had in the van. I started driving again, looking for somewhere to purchase kids' clothes, but nothing was open. It was now dark; the snow was really coming down. The highway was extremely icy, and I had to drive way below the speed limit. Diane changed Jamie's diaper, so at least he was clean. I turned the heat way up, because it was cold outside, and Jamie had no clothes to wear. I mean, he literally had nothing to wear, except his diaper. His clothes and jacket were covered in vomit.

We felt so badly for him, and there was nothing we could really do. Diane sat in the back seat to comfort him while I drove. We finally arrived at the hotel where I was scheduled to perform; I went in to set up. Diane brought James in and held him while I performed. I finished just before 11:30 p.m. We then started on the drive back to Michigan.

We got stuck in a major blizzard just as we neared Chicago's O'Hare Airport. It was so bad that our top speed was 5 MPH…on the freeway! I drove through Wisconsin before letting Diane take over once we got into Illinois. This was another trip from Hell. We were in a blizzard; it was the middle of the night; Jamie was sick, and all of the animals were in the back of the van. It took us almost twelve hours to make it back home. We felt so badly for Jamie every second of the way. The only good news is that he doesn't remember any of it now.

The story didn't end there. We arrived back home at about noon the following day, after driving over twenty hours with no break, except for the 1 ½-hour show I performed. I opened the back of the van to carry the animal crates into our sanctuary. I needed to put them back in their cages and feed them. I noticed the pillowcase that carried our leucistic Texas rat snake was empty. A leucistic animal is one that lacks all pigment, making it solid white with black eyes. I found a hole in the lower right corner, which is how he escaped.

Boo, which is what I named this snake, was gone. I knew he couldn't survive in the van without the heat, because it was below zero outside. I wasn't even sure he was in the van. There was the slim possibility that he escaped in the hotel sometime during my performance in Wisconsin. I figured they would have called, had anyone found him.

There is a happy ending to this story. I carried the last crate into our sanctuary and came back outside to check for Boo one more time. I lifted up a blanket that was near the rear door and found him lying there. I picked him up and noticed how cold he was. I brought him in and immediately placed him inside his cage, where there was a heating pad and a light bulb. I checked on him a couple of hours later and noticed him crawling around like nothing had happened.

All's well that ends well!

Hoodwinked

One of the weirdest rescues I ever did occurred in 2009. I received a phone call from a private owner who had heard about me. I had never met him, but he called and wanted to know if I could help him. I asked him what he needed, and he told me that he had to get rid of a cobra.

I get quite a few calls like this, but the snake usually turns out to be nothing more than a harmless Eastern hognose. I asked him where the snake was, and he said it was in an aquarium in his living room. He told me he had to get rid of it right away, because it had escaped and his girlfriend was worried about their kid's safety. He caught the snake and put it back in its cage, but he didn't know how long it would stay there. I wrote down his address and left right away, after packing up my snake hook, pillow cases and a dog carrier.

I arrived at the entrance to a trailer park and followed the signs, until I located the address he gave me. I knocked on the door and heard kids crying and a dog barking. A man opened the door and told me to come on in. What I saw next blew me away. There was a baby, probably about two-years-old, sitting in one of those walking things on wheels. You place the baby in the center, and he can make it move by moving his legs. There was another boy, about three-years-old, running all over the place. There also an adult terrier running in circles and barking. A lady sitting in the kitchen said, "Hello." There was a large aquarium with fish in the far corner, and right in the middle of the living room was a glass showcase with sliding glass doors.

I approached the showcase and looked in, causing a six-foot cobra to hood up directly in front of me. I couldn't believe this guy actually had a deadly snake like this in a glass cage...in his living room...where his kids were playing...and his dog was running loose. There was no lock on the cage, just a piece of loose duck tape holding the sliding doors together!

I asked the man if he could take his kids, along with the dog, into a bedroom and keep them there while I opened the cage to catch the snake. His wife said she would and took them all away. The man told me his old lady didn't want the snake in their trailer anymore, when she found out what it was. He had told her it was a python, knowing she wouldn't know the difference.

He had to tell her the truth when it escaped, hence the phone call to me. I secured the cobra and placed it into a pillowcase. I then wrapped a couple of rubber bands around the top and placed it inside the dog carrier, just to be safe. I drove it to our sanctuary, where I kept it for a little over two years before finding it a permanent home at a zoo in Missouri.

I find it amazing what some people have in their houses, especially with children or pets around.

Blacklist

   This story is a tribute to Widget, an amazing member of my family who passed away on Christmas morning, 2012. Widget was a black and white ruffed lemur, the largest member in the lemur family and one of the most endangered.

   We raised her in our house since she was only five-months-old. She ate whatever we had for dinner, and she loved to go outside to play on my son's playhouse. She also loved to sit on the pool railing and watch people swim.

   I got her from a friend of mine here in Michigan. Judy owned Widget's parents: "Echo" and

"Snickers." They bred and produced a beautiful baby girl, who Judy named "Widget." Widget was loved by everyone who met her. She never tried to bite and loved being held. I take that back....there was one person who wasn't really fond of her, and I never even got his name.

I ordered a pizza from our favorite place, Mr. Pizza, sometime during the fall of 2001. They were located about one-mile away, and they made the best pizza. They have since gone out of business, but it was great during the short time they were there.

We always had the pizza delivered, since Mr. Pizza had free delivery. It usually arrived in about 45 minutes...they weren't the fastest, just the best! We never use our front door because Widget's huge cage blocked it. It was much easier for us to use the sliding glass door in our kitchen. The glass in the front door, by Widget's cage, is the type where you can see out, but the person on the front porch can't see in…they only see themselves in a mirror. I believe it's called one-way glass.

Anyway, we always let pizza delivery guys know to use the back door, but for some reason, I forgot to tell them when I placed this particular order. I realized this when my dogs started to bark. I got up from the couch in the living room to run to the kitchen door and yell out to come around back. As I exited the living room, I saw the delivery man walk up the steps to the front porch. Remember, I could see him, but he couldn't see in the house.

I failed to tell you that Widget was better than any watch dog. She had a howl that sounded like a ghost wailing. She scared the crap out of everyone! In fact, my step-daughter was awakened one night shortly after moving into the house. She heard Widget screaming and thought our house was haunted!

Back to this story...Widget saw this man coming to the door and started wailing. I couldn't get there fast enough. This guy turned pale and did an about-face. We have five steps leading up to our porch; he cleared all of them with one leap. He jumped off the porch, ran to his car, got in, and floored it backwards down our driveway.

Please don't laugh, because he took our pizza back with him! I received a phone call from Mr. Pizza about ten minutes later asking me what was going on in our house. I had to think quickly, so I told him I have birds, and one of them must have been squawking. He told me they wouldn't deliver to us anymore. I ordered from them again a couple weeks later and had a friend pick up my order. She told me that my name and address were on a piece of paper next to their cash register, with a note saying, "DON'T DELIVER TO THIS ADDRESS!"

I miss my Mr. Pizza, but I really miss Widget the most! Rest in Peace Widget…you were one-of-a-kind and will always be loved and missed!

The King of Hearts

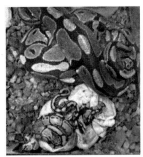

Hatching ball pythons 7/30/2013

I truly hope the message you get out of this story is this: Please realize that life is a precious gift you should always cherish. Never give up hope, because something good might be just around the corner.

Friday night is date night for my wife and me. We were eating dinner at Outback Steakhouse on July 26, 2013. I received a phone call from my neighbor, who lives directly across the street from us. I saw her name on the caller ID and answered it immediately, thinking something had happened to one of our kids. She told me everything was all right at our house, but wanted to know if I could come over because her neighbor had just committed suicide.

I asked which one, and she told me it was the man who lived alone directly behind their house. She said he had multiple snakes and wanted to know if I would come over and get them. One of his friends knew about me and asked if I would help.

I told her I was out with my wife, but I could come over when we got home. I knew the snakes would be fine. I really didn't want to go into his house with the police there, as well as, the clean-up crew. I didn't ask how he did it, nor did I care...I just didn't want to enter a bloody crime scene.

My wife and I went to their house, and they walked us over to the house where the snakes were. I had Diane wait outside, just in case the house was a bloody mess. As I walked up to the porch, a couple of men came outside and greeted me. One was a friend of the deceased; the other was the dead man's father. The dad told me his 51-year-old son had been going through a very rough time and had taken his own life earlier that afternoon.

He had been trying to breed his four ball pythons for years, but never had any success. One of the females laid eggs every year, but none ever hatched. I looked under the hide box in the aquarium and noticed six sunken-in eggs. One of the pythons was coiled around them, but there was no water in the tank, and the eggs looked pretty bad. Eggs need humidity; there was none in this cage.

One of the men helped me carry the aquarium back to our sanctuary where I set everything up the proper way. I decided to leave the eggs with mom...just in case.

I checked on them every morning until a miracle occurred on the sixth night. I entered my sanctuary and noticed one of the eggs starting to hatch! It took three additional days until the final snake emerged, but all six babies eventually hatched.

Hang on…life has lots of surprises just around the corner, and you need to be here to witness them. Just think, maybe this man would still be here today if he had just waited another week and witnessed this miracle. Treasure every day that you are here, and treat every day like it's your last one! If anyone can figure out why I named this chapter "The King of Hearts," please email me at iwantanimalmagic@aol.com. First five correct responses will receive an autographed Animal Magic T-shirt sent to them for free!

Biography

Mark Allen Rosenthal was born June 4, 1962 in Detroit, Michigan and spent the majority of his school years in Oak Park, Michigan. He graduated from Michigan State University in 1984 with a Bachelor of Science degree in Biology and now resides in Belleville, Michigan with his beautiful wife, Diane, and their three wonderful children: Jessica, Samantha & James.

Mark's father introduced him to magic when Mark was eight-years-old. Mark practiced for many years and loved performing for his family. Mark became proficient enough to help pay his way through college. He acquired a job as a magician in 1984 at B'Zar, a very popular nightclub, where he was discovered by a talent agent. He was then hired to perform at the Detroit Tigers 1984 Christmas Party, the year they won the World Series.

Mark was asked to perform at a cousin's birthday party in 1980, and he brought along some of his exotic "pets." The rest, as they say, is history!

Mark was hired by Clayton Environmental Research in Novi when he graduated from college and worked there for two years. He then decided to pursue his lifelong dream of working exclusively with animals. He started The Reptile Source, a reptile wholesale company, and quickly became one of the largest reptile dealers in the United States. He supplied over 1600 pet stores in the early 1990s.

Mark decided to stop wholesaling to pet shops and entertain/educate full time when he saw too many stores selling exotic animals to anyone who could afford them, whether or not they knew what they were doing.

This book is for animal lovers everywhere. Come take a journey back throughout Mark's life, as he relates some of his most memorable stories. He promises you will not only laugh, but shed a few tears, as well.